SKILLS IN RELIGIOUS STUDIES book 2

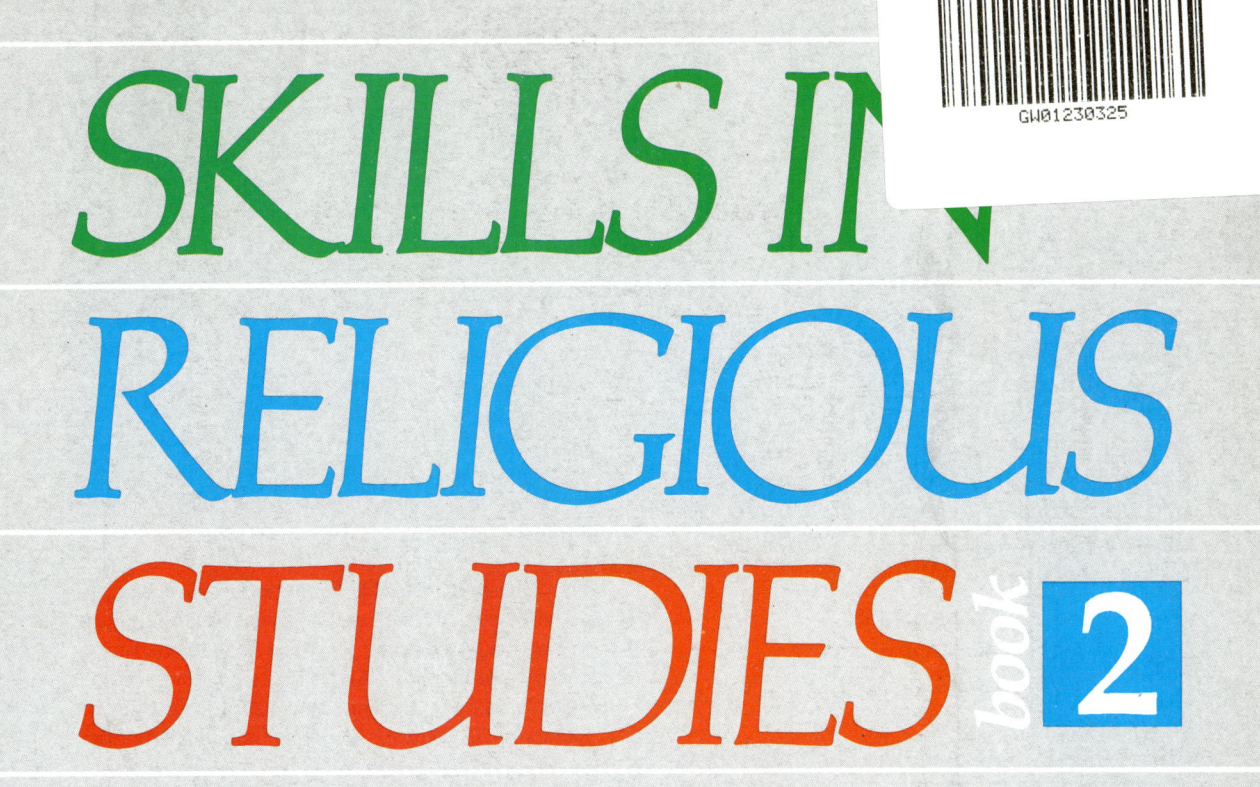

S C MERCIER WITH J FAGEANT

HEINEMANN EDUCATIONAL

Heinemann Educational,
a division of Heinemann Educational Books Ltd,
Halley Court, Jordan Hill, Oxford OX2 8EJ

OXFORD LONDON EDINBURGH MADRID
ATHENS BOLOGNA PARIS MELBOURNE
SYDNEY AUCKLAND SINGAPORE TOKYO
IBADAN NAIROBI HARARE GABORONE
PORTSMOUTH NH (USA)

© S. C. Mercier and J. Fageant 1989

First published 1989
Reprinted 1990
96 97 98 11 10 9 8
British Library Cataloguing in Publication Data

Mercier, S. C.
  Skills in religious studies.
  Bk. 2
  1. Christianity
  I. Title II. Fageant, J.
  200

ISBN 0 435 30201 9

Typeset and illustrated by Gecko Limited, Bicester, Oxon

Printed and bound in Spain by Mateu Cromo

Acknowledgements
Thanks are due to the following for commenting on the manuscript: M.M. Ahsan, Douglas Charing, W. Owen Cole, Sister Ruth Duckworth, Arye Forta, Janey Graham, V.P. (Hemant) Kanitkar, V. Khadke, Peggy Morgan, Saida Rehman, Piara Singh Sambhi and John Snelling.

The Publishers would like to thank the following for permission to reproduce photographs: Mike Abrahams/Network p.54 (bottom); J. Catling Allen Photographic Library p.58 (top), 60; Andes Press Agency/Carlos Reyes p.54 (top); Baptist Union p.27; Barnabys Picture Library pp.12 (centre), 24; Robin Bath pp.38 (bottom), 44 (top), 45 (artist Andy Weber), 47; Bridgman Art Library pp.12 (bottom left), 37, 50; British Library p.36; Buddhist Information Centre p.38 (top); Hans J. Burkard/Bilderberg p.93; J. Allan Cash Ltd p.39; Douglas Dickens p.12 (top); Keith Ellis Collection pp.52, 53; Friends of Neve Shalom p.92; Sally and Richard Greenhill pp.5, 55, 87 (left); Sonia Halliday Photographs pp.26 (top), 35, 56, 58(bottom); Hutchison Library pp.7, 8 (top), 9, 15, 22 (top and bottom), 23 (right), 33, 41, 46, 49, 62, 64 (right), 79, 80 (right), 82, 83, 84, 85, 89, 90; ICOREC p.34 (bottom); Greta Jensen p.42 (bottom); Jewish Education Bureau p.30; The Mansell Collection p.74 (bottom); Maggie Murray/Format p.4 (bottom); NAAS p.4 (top); Christine Osborne Pictures pp.17, 68 (top and bottom), 72, 74 (top); Ann and Bury Peerless Slide Resources and Picture Library pp. 6, 11 (left and right), 12 (bottom), 16, 21, 40, 42 (top), 44 (bottom), 48, 78, 80 (left), 88, 91; David Richardson pp. 10, 14 (bottom), 86, 87 (right); Peter Sanders pp.8 (bottom), 64 (left), 67 (left and right), 69, 70, 73 (top and bottom), 75, 76, 77 (top and bottom); Liz Somerville p.26 (bottom); Swastik Picture House p.20 (left); Homer Sykes p.63; Topham Picture Library p.31; Patrick Ward/Network p.51; Simon Warner p.61 (top); Zefa pp.25, 28 (left and right), 32, 34 (top).
All other photographs supplied by S.C. Mercier.

Cover photographs by: Andes Press Agency/Carlos Reyes (back, left); Douglas Dickens (front, right); ICOREC (front, centre); Ann and Bury Peerless Slide Resources and Picture Library (front, left and back, middle); Peter Sanders (back, right).

Contents

1	Understanding religious believers	4
2	Religious Truth and Revelation	6

Hinduism

3	Hinduism: God within	8
4	Worship in the home	10
5	Shrines and temples	12
6	Community worship	14
7	Serving one another	16
8	Sacred scripture	18
9	Good conquers evil	20

Judaism

10	Judaism: the God of love	22
11	The Word of God	24
12	Keeping the Covenant	26
13	Shabbat	28
14	The synagogue	30
15	Prayer and worship	32
16	Standing firm	34

Buddhism

17	Gotama Buddha	36
18	The Middle Path	38
19	Monks, nuns and lay people	40
20	The shrine	42
21	Buddhism in Britain	44
22	The way things are	46
23	Seasons and festivals	48

Christianity

24	Jesus Christ	50
25	Bread and wine	52
26	Followers	54
27	The Church and churches	56
28	The Bible	58
29	Christian symbols	60
30	The Christian year	62

Islam

31	A plan for all	64
32	The Holy Qur'an	66
33	Five Pillars	68
34	Salah	70
35	The mosque	72
36	The Muslim world	74
37	In the home	76

Sikhism

38	Guru Nanak	78
39	A living Guru	80
40	Community and equality	82
41	A place for worship	84
42	Daily life	86
43	Commitment and courage	88
44	Renewal and celebration	90
45	Room for dialogue	92
	Glossary	94

1 Understanding religious believers

There are many things which are important to us. Food, shelter, warmth and safety are essential. Our home, family and friends are very important too. There will be other things that matter to us. Things we value and the people we love all help to shape us and make us what we are.

Our views, beliefs and attitudes are important. We may inherit the beliefs and values of our family at first. Gradually, we may make the beliefs our own and they become a part of ourselves and the way we look at life. There may be certain beliefs we feel very committed to or ideas we identify with.

People feel strongly about different things. Some people feel very strongly about animal rights or the nuclear issue. Others identify with

B *A woman muslim pilgrim*

A *London marathon runners*

a political party or become committed to a particular lifestyle. There are people who set themselves a personal goal and commit themselves to it (A). Many people are committed to a religious faith and identify with its beliefs and its community of followers (B).

It is sometimes hard to understand the things which are important to other people. An essential skill we need in studying religions is the ability to step into someone else's shoes to try to see things from their point of view. One of the ways in which we can start to do this is by looking at our own experience, the way we feel about things and the beliefs and commitments we have. We can look at what we **value** most, what we **fear** most, what **influences** our thoughts and actions and the **way we live.** If we know what it is like to support a team and to feel a sense of togetherness with other supporters we can try to understand something of the sense of unity religious people experience when they worship together (C). If we know what it feels like when we have let down a friend, we can understand what the religious person feels when they want to ask forgiveness for having let God down. If we

Understanding religious believers

C *Football supporters*

believe it is wrong to kill animals and would prefer to be vegetarian we can appreciate how beliefs can influence diet and daily living. We can even begin to understand the sense of wonder and worship felt by the religious person if we have stood in awe under the night sky and felt the vastness and mystery of the universe and a sense of our own smallness and insignificance.

Of course there are major differences between the experience of the religious person and the experience of the non-believer. It is important to find points of contact and opportunities for sharing experiences and ideas if we are going to try to understand the religions of the world and the people around us.

THINGS TO DO

1. Look at Photo A. How do you think these people prepared in body and mind for the occasion? What would the event mean:
   - to the individual taking part
   - to those watching
   - to family and friends?

   Look at Photo B. How do you think this person has prepared for the occasion? What does the occasion mean for her? Can we tell? Discuss your answers in class.

2. Imagine that the world was going to end tomorrow. What would you do in the next 24 hours? Where would you go and with whom would you want to be? Compare your answers with a friend. Discuss the responses in class. What do they tell us about people's values and commitments?

3. When people feel strongly about something they may express their feelings in words or actions (B and C). Find photographs from old newspapers showing different ways in which people express their beliefs and show their feelings. Make a class display and discuss the different actions, gestures and expressions people show when indicating their beliefs.

4. Looking at the night sky in awe and wonder is not necessarily a religious experience. Many people find that the mystery of the universe makes them wonder about life and its meaning. Describe an occasion when you have felt a sense of wonder or when you have thought about the mystery of time or space or life itself.

5. Draw a diagram or picture, with you represented by a figure at the centre and all the influences around you which make you what you are. Try to draw these in pictures and symbols.

6. In its **Declaration of Human Rights** The United Nations says: 'Everyone has the right to freedom of thought, conscience and religion . . . and freedom, either alone or in community with others and in public or private, to manifest his religion or belief in teaching, practice, worship and observance.' Is this right important? Why? Discuss your ideas in class.

2
Religious Truth and Revelation

The different religions of the world do have things in common. It would be unwise to emphasize only the similarities. Looking at world history and events today, it is clear that there are some very important differences and disagreements between them. Sometimes these are so great that they lead to conflict.

One thing that the religions do share is the fact that they each offer a response to the deeper questions of life such as:
- Where does this life lead?
- What is it all about?
- How should I live my life?

People have been asking questions such as these for thousands of years. Each religious tradition addresses these questions. However, religions have emerged and developed in different times and places. It is not surprising to find that each has its own unique answers to the questions of life.

Each religion is based on the belief that the questions of life have been addressed and that the **Truth** has been made known. Sometimes this Truth is called **Revelation** because it is said to have been revealed, shown or given to humankind. At the heart of each religion is this idea of Truth or Revelation and everything in the faith revolves around it. In some religions the Truth or Revelation is contained in the sacred writings of the faith. In others the Truth is embodied in a person. Often the Revelation or Truth is called **'the Word of God'**.

In Britain there are communities of believers from many different faiths. Christianity arrived with traders in Roman times. There was already a Jewish community settled here shortly after the Norman Conquest. There has been a Muslim community here for 150 years, at first, most of them seamen living in British ports. After World War II Britain was very short of workers. Men and women were recruited from Commonwealth countries to work in industry, in hospitals and on public transport. Many of these people were Christians, others were Muslims, Sikhs, and Hindus. Members of these new communities continued to follow the faith of their families and cultures.

A   *A Hindu shrine in India*

Some people choose a religious path for themselves. This is true of many Buddhists in this country. There are also Buddhists whose family backgrounds are Burmese, Sri Lankan or Vietnamese. Adapting to change has enabled all the religious communities to keep their faith alive in a new and different environment. Each religious community has found new ways of expressing their beliefs as well as preserving the traditions of the past.

THINGS TO DO

1. Look at the two photos in this unit. Make up a set of questions you would need to ask the worshippers in the pictures if you wanted to find out the meaning of what they were doing. Is it possible to work out the answers? What clues are available to help you? What difficulties arise when you cannot ask the people about what their actions mean for them? Discuss this in class.

2. Not all religions are based on a belief in God. **Buddhism**, for example, does not talk about a God. What reasons do people give for believing in God? What arguments are given against this belief? Discuss this in class.

B *A Hindu shrine in Britain*

Religious Truth and Revelation

3. The truth at the heart of a religion remains the same, even though the outward forms and practices may change to adapt to new circumstances. Look at Photos A and B of Hindu shrines. One is in India and the other in Britain. Make a list of the differences. With a partner, discuss the things which may account for the differences between them.

4. What answers have people given to these questions? In pairs write down as many as you can.
   - Where does this life lead?
   - Does it matter how we behave?
   - If so, how should we lead our lives?

   Do you agree with any of these answers? Discuss them in class.

5. Some people follow the religion of their family and culture. Others reject it. Some people are very involved in their religion; others are less committed. Find out about the degree of involvement in religion in your area. Make up six questions about religious belief or practice. For homework get three people to answer your questions. Compare the results.

6. Within all religions we find difference or diversity. For example, we cannot say that all Christians are against the death penalty or that all Hindus are strict vegetarians. Why do you think we find this diversity in a religion? Can you give three examples of diversity within a religion?

3

Hinduism: God within

When Hindus greet one another they bow (A). With hands together they say, 'Namaste'. This means 'I bow to the One within you'. Hindus believe there in One Supreme Spirit of the universe and this spirit is present in everyone. They call the Supreme Spirit **Brahman.** Many Hindus use the word God. According to Hinduism, God can be found in each one of us.

A *The Hindu greeting, 'Namaste'*

B *A sannyasin in a yoga position*

Hindus believe that they can find the presence of Brahman within themselves. For some Hindus the inward journey to Brahman is more important than anything else. They may give up all possessions, personal relationships and desires. Such a person is called a **sannyasin** (B). The sannyasin learns **meditation** and **yoga.** Yoga is an ancient system of exercises for controlling the thoughts and senses. The path of yoga begins with truthfulness, gentleness, respect for all life and self-discipline. It also involves learning how to control one's breathing and exercises to discipline the body and the mind. The goal of the sannyasin is **moksha.** This is when the soul finds perfect union with Brahman.

Most Hindus do not follow the difficult path of the sannyasin. However, they may start the day with meditation. Some Hindus use a **mandala** (C) to help them meditate. The lines draw the eye and mind to the centre of the pattern. This helps to control and quieten the mind. Then the person can ignore distractions and concentrate on finding the stillness and calm within.

Hinduism offers different ways to union with God. Most Hindus follow the path of love or **bhakti.** This takes the form of devotion or worship at a shrine. The shrine may be in the home on a shelf or in the corner of a room (D).

3
Hinduism: God within

C *A yantra or mandala*

It has a picture or an image of a god. Most people have an image in their minds of what God is like, it helps them to pray or to think about God. Hindus use a statue or a picture to help them worship. The image may be a god or a goddess. It is a symbol and a constant reminder of God's presence.

In the Hindu home the day begins with an act of worship at the shrine. Often the mother rises first. She will shower and dress but will not put on shoes; they are not worn in the house. Then she prepares her mind for prayer and approaches the shrine (D). She bows before the image. The presence of God is treasured in the Hindu home and the image is treated like an honoured guest. First it is bathed, with **panchamrit.** This is a mixture of five things: yoghurt, honey, ghee, sugar and milk. Then the image is dressed and anointed with sandalwood paste and coloured powders. Offerings of fresh flowers, food, water and incense are put before the image. The mother then lights a small ghee lamp and holds it up and moves it before the image. She chants hymns of adoration to God and offers her love and service. Acts of devotion at the Hindu shrine are called **puja.**

D *Puja in the home*

THINGS TO DO

1 The first thing one needs to know before entering another culture or learning another language is the greeting. Learn the Hindu greeting. List other greetings you know. Find out their meanings. Make a class poster of different greetings.

2 The shrine is a special place in the Hindu home. It provides a place for turning away from the outside world to think and pray. Do you have a quiet or a special place you like to be in to think or read or daydream or just to be alone? Describe it in words and pictures. If you don't have a special place write about one you would like to have.

3 Gifts can say something which words cannot express. Give three examples when presents are used to say something too deep for words. Discuss them. Hindus place offerings of love before the gods to give thanks for light and food, and for spiritual enlightenment and nourishment too. Draw the offerings given at the Hindu shrine and explain their meaning.

4 What is your mind like? Would you describe it as busy, or full, or muddled? Or is it calm and peaceful? Discuss these things in class. Look at the mandala then draw a mandala of your own design and explain what it is.

5 In pairs, list the different ideas and pictures of God that people have. Is having an image in the mind very different from having an image such as a statue or picture? Discuss.

6 The busy world does not help us to stop and think or be quiet and alone with our own thoughts. Sometimes we hear people speak of the 'inner world'. What do you think this might mean? Design a poster to show the 'inner world' and the 'outside world'.

4
Worship in the home

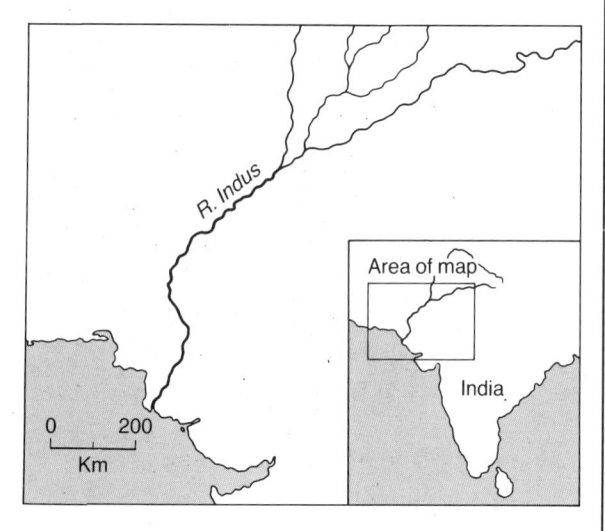

A *Map showing the Indus Valley*

B *Hindu family at worship at the family shrine*

An advanced and prosperous civilization grew up about 4000 years ago in the Indus Valley (A). Gradually, nomadic groups from the north invaded the area and established themselves. They were known as the **Aryans.** The traditions of Hinduism grew out of the meeting of these two cultures. Beliefs, stories, rituals and customs have been passed down from generation to generation. Hinduism has a long and varied history but Hindus believe that the Truth, Brahman, is eternal and existed before time began. The Truth at the heart of a religion remains the same but a religion is a living thing. It finds expression in different times and different places. Hindus in Britain today are finding new ways to express their faith and to adapt to the changing situation.

The Hindu faith is kept alive in the home. Family ties are very important and grandparents often share in the task of bringing up the children in the way of the religion. Hinduism is not just a set of beliefs but it is the way people think, act, eat and carry on their daily lives. The children watch their parents at the shrine and become familiar with the prayers and expressions of **puja** (B). From the images and pictures they learn the stories and symbols of the faith. In the kitchen they learn the rules and beliefs about cleanliness and food. Many Hindus are vegetarian and beef is rarely eaten. The cow is believed to be a sacred animal, it is a symbol of fruitfulness and animals in general are regarded as fellow creatures. Spicy vegetable dishes, pulses, breads and dairy foods are the basic diet in many Hindu homes. Before each meal, the mother offers a portion of the food at the shrine with prayers and thanksgiving. The offering is returned to the meal which then becomes **prashad,** or blessed food.

In the evening the family may pray together at the shrine. Fresh offerings are made, incense stricks are burnt and a small lamp is lit. As hymns are sung the lamp is lifted and moved in a circle in front of the image. This offering of light is called **arti**. Light is a symbol of God's presence and power. It is a reminder that God enlightens the minds of all who turn to him. Everyone receives the power and blessing of light by passing the hands across the flame and over the face and hair.

Many Hindus worship God as a mother. She is **Ambaji** and has many forms. One is the goddess **Durga** who is kind and protective. Another is **Kali** who is fierce and frightening, with extraordinary powers to destroy. Hindus believe that God can be worshipped in many forms. Each image represents an aspect of God's nature and power. Hindus know that no image can be great enough to represent God completely (C).

4 Worship in the home

C *Mother goddess Ambaji, Durga (right) and Kali (left)*

THINGS TO DO

1. Look at Photo B of the shrine. What is happening? Write a set of 10 questions you would like to ask the family if you were invited to visit. Discuss the questions in class. Which ones can you answer and which ones are more difficult without speaking to a Hindu?

2. Hindus believe that every living creature has a soul. Like people, animals have a right to life. Many people are vegetarian nowadays. What reasons do people have for not eating meat? In a group, prepare a debate on vegetarianism for a TV programme.

3. Many Hindu mothers go to work during the day, some have professional jobs, others prefer to put all their energy into bringing up the family. They also play an important part keeping the Hindu faith alive in the home. Write an account called 'A Day in the Life of a Hindu Home' using the text to help you. It can be from the point of view of the mother or another member of the family.

4. Read the prayer to the mother goddess. What qualities does a mother possess? Is the image of the mother a suitable one for God? In what ways is it different from speaking of God as a father? Discuss these questions in class. Write your own version of a prayer a Hindu might say to God as mother.

Hindu prayer to the Mother Goddess

Oh Mother Supreme,
The power behind all that is and moves;
The little insect or reptile, bird or beast,
man or woman, all these are your children.
You love them, protect them and care for them.
The grass, shrubs and trees are all yours.
You spread your wings to discipline the sun,
the moon, stars and planets. The four elements –
you control them too.
Your power is bewildering:
How great are you
and how small am I.

5. India is often portrayed as a land of poverty. Yet it has great wealth in terms of religion, history and culture as well as its achievements in the modern world. Collect newspaper cuttings which show Britain having problems with housing, unemployment and poverty. Find pictures which show Britain's riches, its history, culture and wealth today. Compare the two images of Britain. Which is correct? Should we rethink our images of countries such as India?

6. Without using words how would you show your feelings in the following situations?
   - When an important person enters the room.
   - When you want to say 'thank you'.
   - When you get ready for a best friend or close relative who is coming to stay.

   Compare these expressions with the expressions of devotion in Hindu worship.

5 Shrines and temples

In India, the Hindu temple is a house for a god or goddess (A). It contains a shrine with an image of the deity. There is a priest to take care of the images. Worshippers go to the temple, just as they might visit a close friend or go to see an important person. They may stop to leave an offering or to pray or express their devotion by walking reverently round the image. In the villages of India many shrines are in the open air and the local people care for them. According to the Hindu scriptures, any offering no matter how humble, is acceptable to God as long as it is given with sincerity and love.

There are Hindu temples in Britain too, some are purpose built, some are converted halls and churches (B). In a Hindu temple in Britain there are several shrines dedicated to different gods. **Vishnu** is represented at most temples; he is the saviour of the world and has taken many forms. He has appeared on earth as prince **Rama** and as the Lord **Krishna.** God is also represented in the form of **Shiva** (C). Shiva is often seen as a mystic, deep in meditation, with a cobra and a trident at his side. Shiva is also the Lord of destruction and death and controls the heartbeat of the universe with his drum.

Most Hindu temples in Britain have a shrine to the mother goddess and another to **Ganesha** (C). Ganesha is an important image for many Hindus. He has the head of a wise elephant, he is kindly and approachable and is seen as the remover of obstacles. Hindus pray to him first, asking him to remove those thoughts and feelings that stand in the way of worship. The shrines are usually at one end of a large hall. This is where the congregation gathers for worship. The worshippers sit on the carpet on the floor, below the level of the shrines.

A *A Hindu temple in India*

B *A Hindu temple in Britain*

C *Images of Shiva (left) and Ganesha (right)*

Shrines and temples

In Britain, the temple has become the focal point for the Hindu community. Older members can meet friends from a similar cultural background who may share the same customs and languages. The temple may run a youth club for its teenagers. Most young Hindus here are born British. They have Gujurati, Punjabi or another Indian language as their mother tongue. English becomes their first language at school, so they may not learn to read and write their home language. Many Hindu temples offer classes where they can learn to do so. In these ways the Hindu community meets the needs of its members.

Friendship, hospitality and service to others are important for Hindus. Volunteers at the temple provide transport, take classes, clean, prepare food and also raise money for charities (D). In many ways the temple serves the community at large and welcomes visitors and provides opportunities for people to gain a greater understanding of the Hindu faith.

THINGS TO DO

1. Caves and mountains in India are holy places. Hindu temples in India often reflect the shape of mountain tops and caves. At the heart of the temple is the god or goddess. Entering the temple is symbolic of entering the depths of one's own heart and finding God there. Draw a diagram of the Indian temple and write about its shape, symbolism and purpose.

2. Look at the photos. Compare the Indian temple with the Hindu temple in Britain. Can you think of reasons for the differences? Discuss these in class.

3. Many Hindu families in Britain have their origins in India. There are Hindus, too, from the Caribbean and Africa. The Hindu temple serves the whole community. Imagine you are a Hindu. Write a letter to a friend in India telling them about your local temple here.

4. Look at the timetable for the week in a temple in Britain (Illustration D). Design a poster to inform Hindus living in the area about the activities and services offered at their local temple.

5. Imagine you are the mayor for a city with a large Hindu community. Write a letter to the temple expressing your appreciation of the contribution of the Hindu community in the life of the city.

6. Hindus believe that God can be found in the hearts and minds of people. What would you look for in the life of a person to see if God were at work there? Write down your ideas and discuss them in class.

ANYTOWN HINDU TEMPLE + COMMUNITY CENTRE ACTIVITIES

MONDAY
Elderly Day Centre: Recital of Scriptures / Arti — 10.15 – 11.30 am
Lunch — 12 noon

TUESDAY
Ladies Circle: Fundraising for Charity Coffee morning — 10. – 11.30 am
After school Club: Games and Puzzles — 3.15 – 4.30 pm

WEDNESDAY
Elderly Day Centre: Card games and coffee — 10. – 11.30 am

THURSDAY
Mothers & Toddlers: Play group — 10. – 12 noon
After school club older children: Yoga classes — 6 – 8 pm

FRIDAY
Elderly Day Centre: Puja & Arti — 11 – 1 pm
After school club: Storytelling — 3.15 – 4 pm

SATURDAY
Classes: Hindi, Gujurati, Punjabi — 9 – 12 noon
All welcome: Arti — 6 pm

SUNDAY
All welcome: Arti service / Lunch — 11 am – 12.30 pm / 1 pm.

D *Timetable of activities at a Hindu cultural centre*

6
Community worship

The priest at the Hindu temple who leads the worship is usually a learned man, able to read **Sanskrit**, the ancient language of the Hindu scriptures. A priest must come from a family of priests. Every temple has a priest to care for and prepare the images for worship.

Many Hindu temples in Britain hold a regular **arti** service (A). Worshippers come to receive the offering of light and to pray (B). Before going into the shrine room they remove their shoes. This keeps the carpets clean to sit on and is a sign of respect. On entering, the worshippers bow, showing reverence to the gods. Usually they approach the shrine to Ganesha first and then each of the other deities. Each image at the temple represents an aspect of God's nature and power.

As the worshippers bow before the deity they may leave an offering of milk, fruit, food, flowers or money at the shrine. They may whisper a few words of prayer and touch the foot of the steps or platform on which the image stands. Men and women sit separately but there is no religious reason for this.

Worship often begins with the singing of hymns or **bhajans**, accompanied by the musicians on the harmonium and tabla or drums. The priest attends to the deities. He will have first prepared himself, bathed and put on clean clothes. The images are washed and dressed and anointed with yellow turmeric and red kumkum and sandalwood paste. The priest arranges a tray with offerings of water, food, rice, flowers, a fan, incense, a small bell and a conch shell (C). Also on the tray is the lit arti lamp filled with ghee. The priest presents each offering in turn to the deities reciting words from the scriptures.

Finally he lifts up the arti lamp before the images. He moves the light in a circle in front of each god and goddess. The people stand, clapping to the music. The singing gets louder, the conch shell is blown like a trumpet and the congregation joins in with bells and drums. There is a sense of excitement as if an

A *Offerings of light at the temple*

B *Worshippers receiving the light*

honoured guest were being received. Then the priest turns to face the congregation and moves the lamp again. It is taken round the worshippers. Everyone receives the light, its power and energy and asks God to purify and enlighten their mind (B).

At the end of the service, **prashad** is shared out. This is food, which has been offered to the gods. It is a symbol of God's blessing to all who join in this act of love and worship.

Arti is the most popular service. On some special occasions there is a ceremony called **havan**. A special fire is lit in a container. Fire is an ancient symbol for God. It was once the receiver of sacrifices, presents offered to gods. Today the offerings are incense, rice and sandalwood which are sprinkled on the flames. The smoke carries the hymns and prayers to heaven.

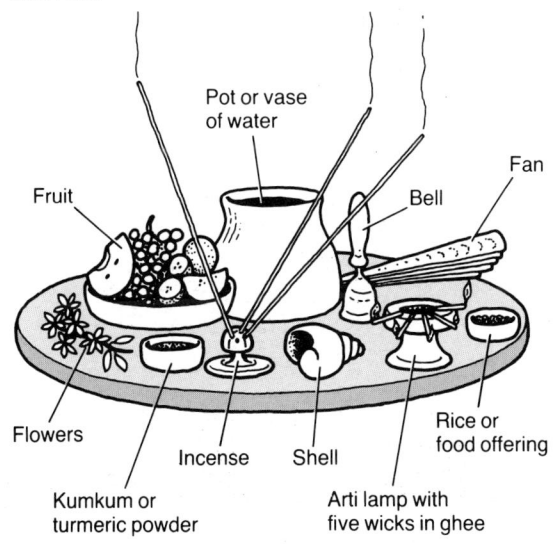

C *The arti tray*

THINGS TO DO

1. The arti tray contains five symbols for the five **elements**. Five senses are also represented as God is to be worshipped with all the senses. Draw the symbols on the tray. Identify and explain what they stand for. Say how the symbols are used in worship.

6
Community worship

2. A person's religion is often an essential part of their identity. It is good to be in a place where your beliefs, identity and culture are valued and regarded as important. Why is this? How can we show that we value the religions and cultures of others as well as our own? Make a list of ways in which this can be done in school.

3. Hindus do not worship the images. They worship God. God's power is shown in images, symbols and pictures. Design your own symbols to represent the following:
   - strength
   - all-seeing power
   - healing powers
   - love
   - peace
   - generosity

4. Many Hindu temples in Britain have to stay locked up when there is no one to keep guard. There are problems with vandalism. Some Hindus feel that their religion and culture is under attack. Design a poster with the slogan 'Let us Pray' which demands that all members of our society have the freedom to worship in peace.

5. Light is an important symbol. Draw the arti lamp and write a hymn thanking God for the gift of light, or a poem on the symbol of light.

6. Gestures, positions of the body and facial expression tell us about the experience and beliefs of the worshipper. We can understand some of these as they are familiar in other situations. Discuss the meaning of:
   - bowing
   - putting hands together
   - clapping
   - 'receiving' light
   - offering gifts

   What do they tell us about the beliefs and feelings of the worshippers?

7
Serving one another

According to the Hindu scriptures there are several ways to **moksha** or union with God. There is the path of yoga and meditation and there is the path of love, worship and devotion. There is a third path, the way of unselfish action. This means doing one's duty in life patiently and without wanting any reward. It means doing one's daily work without complaint and to the best of one's ability, dedicating every action to God.

Hinduism teaches that everyone has a duty or **dharma**. Dharma means law, religious duty or simply 'what is right'. Dharma refers to the laws which govern the universe as well as the duties of each individual. A person's dharma depends on their family, their job, their age and their abilities. The most popular teaching on dharma is the story of **Rama** (A).

Long ago, in India there lived an obedient son and heir to the throne. However, his father had promised his wife two wishes. Envious of Rama's position, she demanded that he be exiled for 14 years and her own son be crowned instead. The old king died. Rama knew that it was his duty (dharma) to keep his father's promise even though everyone wanted him to be king. So he went into exile. During his time in the forest, Rama overcame the forces of evil and destroyed the demon Ravana who threatened the peace of the world. After 14 years Rama returned to be crowned with his wife Sita. As king and ruler, Rama's duty was to serve his people to the best of his ability and to establish peace and justice in his kingdom. Throughout his reign Rama put his people's welfare before his own and set an example of perfect obedience to dharma.

Born a prince, Rama belonged to the ruling class. Hindu society was originally divided into four classes. These are called **varnas**. Families in the priesthood belonged to the **Brahmin** class. Royalty and those serving in government or in the army were **Kshatriyas**. People in business or trade were **Vaishyas**. Labourers belonged to the **Shudra** class. According to the scriptures, the four varnas were brought into being at creation. Everyone was given a sacred duty to perform, in order to ensure that the needs of the community were served. Other groups grew up in Hindu society according to family and occupation. These are known as **jati(s)** or **castes**. Some jobs were believed to be unclean. People in these jobs were considered to be outside the caste system and labelled **untouchables** (B). In the villages of India the caste system remains rigid. In towns and cities and among those who live in Britain the caste system has lost much of its hold.

A *Image of Rama at a Hindu shrine*

7
Serving one another

B *An 'untouchable'*

Untouchables in India have demanded a just system to give them equal rights, and the laws have changed but the prejudice against them remains.

THINGS TO DO

1. Make a list of the new vocabulary in this unit. Explain and write out the meaning of each word so that it makes sense to you. Check your definitions with a friend.

2. What do you think are the duties of the following people?
   - a mother
   - a father
   - a school pupil
   - a farmer
   - a police officer

   Discuss these questions in pairs:
   - Do you think we all have a duty in life?
   - Do we know what it is? How?

   Share your ideas in class.

3. Rama found that doing his duty often meant sacrificing his own happiness for the good of others. Is this always true of doing one's duty? Look at examples with which you are familiar. Discuss your answers in class.

4. Caste in India prevented the untouchables from moving up in the world. In Britain divisions in our society make it hard for some people to get on. What are the reasons for this? Can you give examples? Can we make sure that there is equal opportunity for all in our society? Discuss these questions in class.

5. Rama is the model of righteousness. Hindus try to follow his example of perfect duty and unselfish service to others. Look at Photo A. Imagine you are a Hindu before the shrine of Rama. Write a prayer to Rama asking for help to follow his example.

6. The name Hinduism goes back to the time of the Muslim rule in India and was used to distinguish native Indians from the ruling people. Hindus call their religion **Eternal Dharma**. Discuss why Hindus feel this is a better name for their faith.

8
Sacred scripture

In Photo A, the priest is reciting verses from the scriptures. The oldest Hindu scriptures are the **Vedas**. It is believed the words were heard by the holy men of ancient India. The Vedas contain hymns to the Gods. They also contain teachings about Brahman. They are written in the ancient language of Sanskrit. Most Hindus are more familiar with the **Ramayana** and the **Mahabharata**. These epic stories have been passed down from generation to generation through poetry, song, dance and drama.

The Mahabharata is about a war between two families: there was once a king of India called **Pandu**. He gave up his throne to live as a sannyasin and asked his brother to rule in his place and be like a father to his sons. King Pandu's sons, the **Pandavas**, were renowned for their virtue and courage. They were the rightful heirs to the throne. Their evil cousins, the **Kauravas**, robbed them of their inheritance and tricked them out of their land. Having tried all peaceful means to establish justice and freedom for their people, the sons of Pandu were forced into battle against the Kauravas.

One of the sons of Pandu, **Arjuna**, was a skilled and courageous warrior (B). He was to lead his brothers into war. As the battle lines

A   *The priest in the temple, using the scriptures*

KRISHNA AND ARJUNA

B   *Krishna and Arjuna on their chariot, at the battle front*

were drawn up, Arjuna was filled with horror at the thought of shedding the blood of his cousins. He turned to his charioteer, **Krishna**. Krishna told Arjuna that it was his duty as prince and warrior to fight for justice and freedom. He told him he must go to battle without any wish for selfish gain, without any personal hatred or bitterness. He should fight for his people and for justice and righteousness. This was his dharma. Krishna's sermon is called the **Bhagavad Gita**, the Song of the Lord. At the end of the hymn it is revealed that Krishna is God in human form.

The Bhagavad Gita is the best loved of the scriptures. In it, Krishna explains that the soul is eternal. He says it casts off the body at death like old clothes and takes on a new body. Krishna also speaks about the different ways to God. He says that whoever loves him above all else will find **moksha**. The words of the Bhagavad Gita are treasured by Hindus and in some temples the book is placed in a shrine to show reverence and respect for its teachings.

8
Sacred scripture

There are many other stories about Krishna in the **Puranas**. These tell of his youth as a cowherd. He used to play his flute in the forest and the milkmaids all fell in love with him. One girl was especially dear to Krishna. She was called **Radha**. The devotion between them is a symbol of the love between God and the human soul.

THINGS TO DO

1. Look at Photo A. What can you see? How can we tell that these are sacred scriptures? How is the priest using them? Discuss these questions then write an interview with the priest about the scriptures.

2. In the Bhagavad Gita, Krishna says he comes to earth at different times to save mankind whenever the powers of evil get too strong. What things need to be put right in the world? Do we need help? What help is available? How would a religious person respond to this question? Discuss your answers.

3. The Pandavas tried every possible peaceful means to defeat evil. Eventually they had no alternative but to fight for justice. Is war sometimes right? Are some things more important than human life? These are difficult questions. Write down your own thoughts first then discuss them in class.

4. Krishna said the soul is eternal. Draw a diagram to show the cycle of birth, life, death and rebirth, and explain it.

5. Hindu children can read the Mahabharata in comic strip form. Design a front page for a comic on the Mahabharata showing the evil Kauravas, the five courageous sons of Pandu, and Krishna.

6. In the Bhagavad Gita the Lord Krishna said, 'Even those who worship other gods with love . . . do really worship me.' What do you think this means? What does it tell us about Hinduism?

C *Kauravas and Pandavas*

9

Good conquers evil

A *Janamashtami celebrations at the temple*

B *Krishna as a child*

Festivals are important in Hinduism. Most festivals focus on a particular god or goddess. **Navaratri** or Nine Nights is a festive time for all Hindus. The celebrations are dedicated to the mother goddess. Some Hindus especially remember the story of the goddess Durga slaying the buffalo demon and her image is the centre of worship at this time. On the tenth day is **Dassehra**. This is a popular festival. In northern India it is dedicated to Rama and in western India it celebrates the story of the sons of Pandu. All these stories tell of right conquering wrong and remind people that real power is not to be found in physical might or weapons.

Following Dassehra is the festival of lights called **Divali**. It is dedicated to **Lakshmi**, the goddess of good fortune.

These are autumn and winter festivals. In spring the festival of **Holi** is celebrated with splashes of colour and playful tricks. In the summer the main festival is **Janamashtami**, which is Krishna's birthday (A). Krishna was born at midnight. Many Hindus fast for the day and remember the story of Krishna.

There was once a demon king who ruled over his people with threats of murder and violence. His name was **Kamsa**. Kamsa had been warned that his sister **Devaki** and her husband **Vasudeva** would have a child who would overthrow him and bring in a reign of righteousness. To avoid taking any risks, Kamsa had each of their children murdered as soon as they were born. By the time the eighth child was due Kamsa had put Devaki in prison under guard. So the child Krishna was born in the dungeons (B). Vasudeva knew the child was destined to save the world. He crept past the sleeping guards with the baby wrapped up, in a basket. He went out into the stormy night to find a home for the child. As he crossed the raging waters of the river Yamuna it seemed to want to reach up to touch the baby. One leg of the child dangled into the water and immediately the waves retreated and Vasudeva crossed with the baby unharmed. He left the child in the safety of a farmer's cottage next to the farmer's sleeping wife.

Krishna grew up surrounded by love. He looked after his stepfather's cattle in the forest.

Good conquers evil

Eventually he returned to the palace and destroyed the demon Kamsa. The people crowned him as king. Krishna is recognized as God in human form and his birthday is a special occasion. Pictures of the baby Krishna are displayed in homes and temples. His image is decorated with garlands of flowers (C). Some temples build a cradle for the image of the baby Krishna and hold an arti ceremony. Prashad and festive foods are shared. Festivals are occasions to remember God's presence and protection, to give thanks and to celebrate together.

C *Krishna's shrine*

3 At Janamashtami the temple is packed and friends and relatives meet (A). Everyone wears their best clothes. People put offerings of food and flowers before the images. There are musicians and sometimes the stories of Krishna are told in dance. Imagine you are celebrating the birthday of Krishna. Describe how you prepare for and celebrate the festival.

4 If God can be worshipped in the image of a small helpless child, what does this tell us about the Hindu idea of God? Discuss this and try to explain your answers in writing.

5 Read the Gayatri Mantra below. Design a Hindu greetings card for one of the festivals. Put the Gayatri Mantra inside. It is a well loved prayer recited by most Hindus every day.

> **Gayatri Mantra**
>
> Oh God, creator and Life Giver
> of the Universe; everywhere
> and in all things,
> We meditate on your splendour
> and Divine Light and
> pray for purity of mind
> and knowledge of the truth.

6 The symbol **Om** or **Aum** in Illustration D is a sacred sound used in meditation. It stands for the Eternal Truth. Design a poster using this symbol and other pictures, symbols or words to communicate what you have learnt about Hinduism.

D *Om or Aum*

THINGS TO DO

1 Draw a circle to represent the year and mark in the different seasons with pictures. Put in the Hindu festivals, marking them with pictures or symbols. Can you add others?

2 Tell the story of the birth of Krishna in words and pictures, as if for a children's picture book. The stories about Krishna's childhood are intended to inspire love and devotion.

10
Judaism: The God of love

A   The Mezuzah

When visiting a Jewish home you will find a clue as to the religion of the household right at the front door. On the door post is a Mezuzah (A). The Mezuzah is a tiny scroll of parchment. Sometimes it is kept in a small cover or container. Written on parchment are verses in Hebrew from the **Torah**, the most sacred of the Jewish scriptures. The verses begin the Jewish prayer called the **Shema**: 'Hear O Israel, the Lord your God is One . . .'. The Mezuzah is a symbol and reminder of the teachings of the Torah and the love of God.

Jews believe in one God. They also believe that they belong to a kind of large family, the family of **Israel**. This family has a long story. It begins with two characters. One of them is God. The other is **Abraham**. Abraham was the head of a tribe. He is sometimes called the father of the people of Israel. God wanted to talk to people. He wanted them to know and love him. He was looking for someone who would listen.

Abraham was searching too. He longed to find God and talk with him. He wanted a home and a future for his people. When Abraham and God sought and found each other they came to an agreement. Abraham showed God that he was willing to obey him in all things. God asked him to offer his son as a sacrifice. But when Abraham prepared to kill and offer his son God stopped him. Abraham had shown that he would sacrifice everything for God. He had shown absolute obedience. So God promised that he would make him the father of a great people. They would live in a land they could call their own: the land of **Canaan**. This promise between God and the family of Israel was called the **Covenant**.

Israel grew and became a nation. A new covenant was needed. This time God spoke with Moses on **Mount Sinai** (B). God had rescued his people from slavery in Egypt. Moses took them through the desert to begin their journey to the **Promised Land**. In the desert the people began to rebel and wanted to return to Egypt. God saw that Israel needed guidelines if they were going to be partners in a covenant with him. God revealed the holy Torah to Moses on Mount Sinai. The Torah was God's word, his promise and his commandment. The Torah sealed the relationship between God and Israel like a

B   Mount Sinai

10

Judaism: The God of love

marriage vow. It bound Israel to God in a special agreement. If they were to be God's people they must be holy like God and separate themselves from false worship, evil, murder, greed, theft, envy, dishonesty and gossip. In return, God promised that they would again live in their own land under his care and protection. The Torah was a precious gift. Like a wedding ring it was a symbol of a promise of love and faithfulness. In their daily lives Jews try to keep their covenant with God, and remember his love and protection.

THINGS TO DO

1. Look up the words of the Shema in a Bible. (The Christian Bible contains some of the Jewish scriptures which Christians call the **Old Testament**.) The verses are from *Deuteronomy* chapter 6 verses 4–9, chapter 11 verses 13–21 and *Numbers* chapter 15 verses 37–41. What does it tell us about the beliefs of Judaism? In what ways must Jews remember God?

2. Draw a Mezuzah scroll and its holder. Most Jewish households have one on the doorpost of each of the main rooms in the house. Some Jews touch the Mezuzah as they enter the house. Imagine you are from a Jewish family. A friend you take home asks about the Mezuzah. Say what it is and why it is important. Write this explanation under your drawing.

3. Read the story of God's covenant with Abraham in *Genesis* chapter 22 verses 1–19. Act out the story in a group. Discuss the meaning of the story. Do you think that following a religious way of life means making big sacrifices? What sort of sacrifices?

4. Revise the Passover story. Then look at the story of Mount Sinai in *Exodus* chapters 19 and 20. What things in the story point to the importance of the Covenant? Tell the story as if you were writing it for Jewish children in words and pictures.

5. The **Ten Commandments** (*Exodus* chapter 20) are sometimes called the **Ten Sayings** because the first is not really a commandment. It has been said that they can be summed up in 'love God and love your neighbour as yourself'. Do you think this is correct? Discuss this in class.

6. Israel is the name given to the Jewish people in their scriptures. Israel is sometimes described as God's bride. Read the text again. Why do you think that Israel is described as being like a bride? Explain in a short paragraph.

C Jewish rabbi writing Hebrew

11
The Word of God

The Torah in Photo A is the scroll used in the **synagogue** where Jews gather for worship. It is called the **Sefer Torah** (A). The text is in Hebrew (B). It contains five books or texts: *Genesis, Exodus, Leviticus, Numbers* and *Deuteronomy*. These are called the **books of Moses**. According to Jewish tradition, when God gave Moses the Torah he also explained it. So Moses received both the Torah and its interpretation. Therefore every page of the Torah has the text and its commentary. This is because the meaning of the text is not always clear as the teachings and laws need to be interpreted for different times and situations. The words of famous **rabbis** who devoted their lives to the study and interpretation of the Torah were remembered and written down. These collected discussions are contained in the **Talmud**. The commentaries alongside the text of the Torah draw on the interpretations of the Talmud, and bring the word of the Torah to life.

The Torah is the **word of God** for all Jews, and the Sefer Torah in the synagogue is a symbol of the living word of God. The scroll is handled with reverence and care. The manuscript itself is handwritten on parchment. As there can be no mistakes in the text it takes time and great patience on the part of the scribe who copies it out. It is an act of love and worship in itself.

The Sefer Torah is rolled on two wooden poles with handles. These are called the **Trees of Life.** In most synagogues the scroll is wrapped in an embroidered mantle and crowned in silver and given a silver breastplate. The scrolls of the Torah are kept in a special cupboard called the holy **Ark** or, in Hebrew, **Aron Hakodesh**. When the Torah is read a **yad** or pointer is used to avoid touching the text. During the service at the synagogue the Sefer Torah is taken around the congregation in a procession. People lean forward to kiss the mantle or they may touch it with their prayer shawl and then kiss the shawl (C). After the reading the Torah is lifted up for all to see. This

A *Sefer Torah, the mantle and text*

ceremony of seeing, touching and holding is an expression of love and devotion to the word of God.

The Torah is the most important part of the Jewish scriptures but it is not the whole of them. There are also the words of the prophets and the writings of historians and other learned Jews. These are contained in the **Tenakh**. The word Tenakh comes from the three Hebrew letters for **Torah, Nevi'im** and **Ketuvim**. These are the five books of Moses, the Prophets and the Writings. The Tenakh is usually a book rather than a scroll. It is sometimes called the **Bible** or the **Holy Scriptures**.

B *The Hebrew alphabet*

C *Leaning forward to kiss the mantle*

11
The Word of God

> THINGS TO DO

1. The Torah is in **Hebrew**. This ancient language is still spoken. Jewish children learn the alphabet at a young age. The letters go from right to left. Look at Illustration B, then write out the Hebrew alphabet.

2. Make a small model of the scroll of the Sefer Torah.

3. When something is very precious to us we treat it differently from other things. The Torah is very precious. Imagine you are Jewish. Make a leaflet for children with words and pictures to show the ways in which the Torah is treated as precious and holy.

4. The Talmud is important for understanding the text of the Torah. It is the work of very learned rabbis. It contains the **Mishnah**, the interpretation of the meaning of the law and **Gemara**, the discussions on the Mishnah. Working in groups, do your own interpretation and discussion on the meaning for today of:
   (a) *Exodus* chapter 20 verse 8,
   (b) *Exodus* chapter 20 verse 12,
   (c) *Deuteronomy* chapter 19 verse 21 and *Leviticus* chapter 19 verses 17–18.
   Discuss your interpretations in class.

5. Every year there is a festival called **Simchat Torah**. It celebrates the gift of the Torah. The synagogue readings for the year end and begin again at *Genesis* on this occasion. It is a time for great rejoicing and the Sefer Torah is taken in procession around the synagogue. Design a poster inviting Jews to join the celebrations at the synagogue.

6. Look at the photos in this unit. Imagine you are interviewing one of the members of the synagogue. Write a sequence of questions and answers about what is happening in these scenes.

12 Keeping the Covenant

A *A boy wearing the tallit and tephillin*

The boy in Photo A is reading prayers from the Holy Scriptures of Judaism. He is following the commandments in the Torah regarding daily prayer. He is wearing the **tallit** or prayer shawl and **tephilin**. Tephilin are two small boxes with leather straps, which contain parchments with passages from the Torah. One of these is tied to the weaker (usually left) arm and the other is fixed on the forehead. Tallit and tephilin are worn by Jewish men for prayer during the week. In this way men keep the covenant and obey God's holy commandments.

There are many ways in which Jews obey the Torah in their home and daily lives. If religion is concerned with every part of human life then it must be concerned with what a person eats. The Torah commands Jews to eat only foods which are 'fit' or **kosher** (B). Only animals with cloven hooves and which chew the cud are 'fit' to eat and only domesticated fowl are kosher.

All meat must be clean and free from blood. The Jewish community therefore has its own butchers who make sure that the commandments are kept when the animals are slaughtered. Shell fish and fish without fins and scales are not acceptable. Milk and meat products are kept separate and a time lapse between eating meat and milk is necessary. Some households keep separate cutlery and china for meat and milk foods.

Buying Kosher food in Britain is not always easy (B). Prepared Kosher foods in tins and boxes are marked in Hebrew but the Jewish mother has to take care in preparing her family's food to see that it is kosher. In keeping God's commandments every time they eat, Jews are reminded several times a day of their relationship with God. This essential part of daily life is, therefore, holy. At every meal Jews give thanks to God by saying a simple blessing which may begin: 'Blessed are you O Lord of the Universe who has given us . . .'. There are different blessings for every kind of food.

Some prayers said in the Jewish home are formal. They are said at certain times and they are often psalms or hymns from the scriptures.

B *Kosher foods*

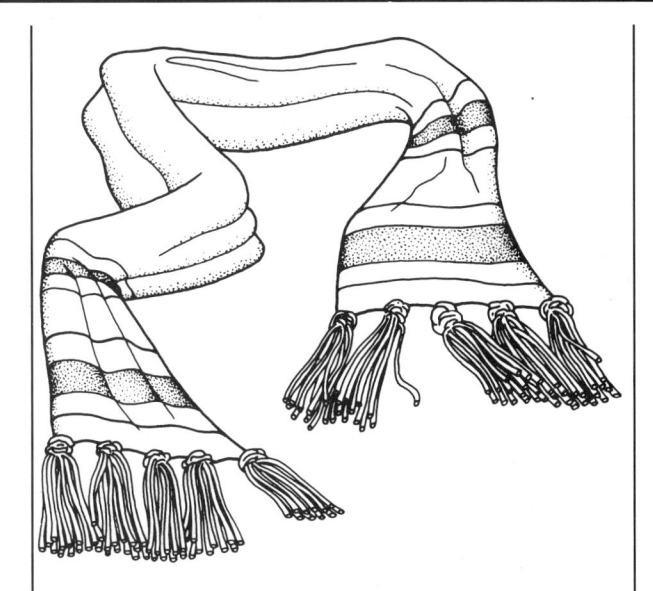

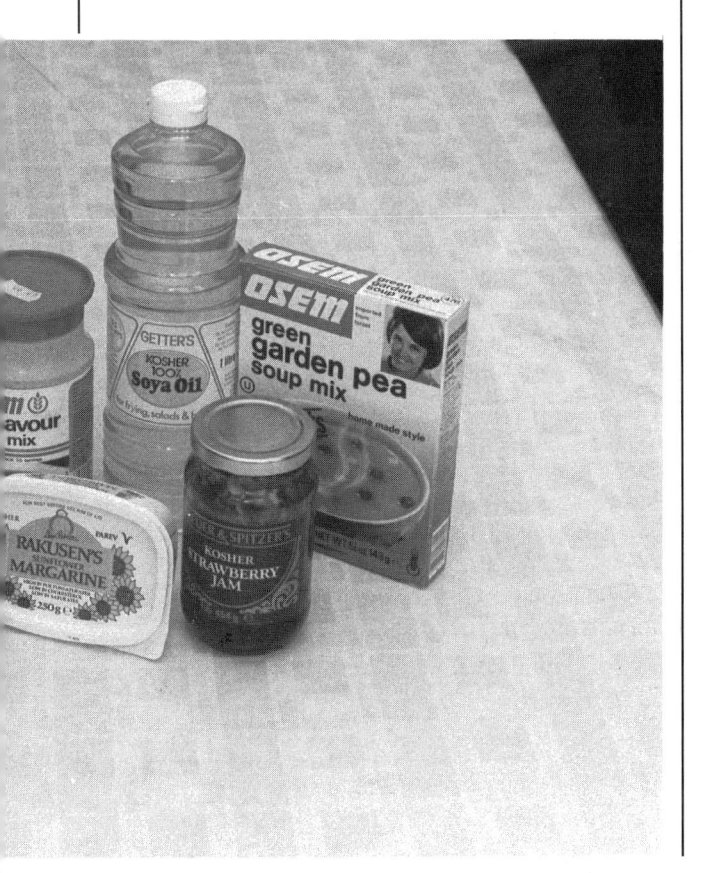

12
Keeping the Covenant

C *A tallit*

Other prayers are informal. They might be prayers of happiness and thanks or prayers for saying sorry or simple requests for help and guidance. The words can be made up and said at any time. In all these ways Jewish people remember God, keep his commandments and communicate with him in their everyday lives.

THINGS TO DO

1. Look at Illustration C. Make a small tallit out of cloth or paper and cotton thread. It should be white with a blue cord running through it (*Numbers* chapter 15 verses 37–39). Each tassle should have three short strands of white and one which is left long to wind around the other strands. To knot the tassle, tie a double granny knot close to the material. Wind the longer strand round the others seven times then double knot all the strands again. Then wind the long strand again eight times, double knot again, wind 11 times, tie another double granny knot and wind 13 times and finish off with a double granny knot. Make a label to explain who wears a tallit, when and why it is worn.

2. Jewish parents must teach the commandments to their children. Find out more from the commandments about food (*Leviticus* chapter 11). Make a poster, with pictures on kosher laws, which a parent could put up in the kitchen for children to see.

3. The laws of the covenant are important for the individual. They are also important for binding the community together. How does keeping certain laws and customs bind people together? Which habits, rules, customs and symbols bind your school together as a community? Discuss this in class.

4. Some Jews think that there are laws and practices which are no longer relevant or meaningful. Some Jews keep a strict kosher kitchen, others do not. What are the dangers of giving up certain traditions of a religion? What are the arguments for change? Discuss these questions in class.

5. Invite a Jewish mother to describe how she keeps the commandments in her home and kitchen. Write about keeping a kosher kitchen from the point of view of a Jewish mother or child.

6. Jewish men usually wear a **yamulkah** (kippur or kappel) on their heads. Covering the head is a sign of respect before God. Find out about ways in which people of all faiths express their respect before God when they pray or worship. Show the information on a chart with illustrations.

13
Shabbat

A *The mother says the blessing*

B *The Shabbat table*

The Jewish week revolves around the Sabbath. In Hebrew it is called **Shabbat**. Sometimes it is called **Shabbes**. Every Jewish household keeps Shabbat in its own way. However, there are some Shabbat traditions which are always the same. In the Torah Jews are told to keep Shabbat holy. It must be a day of rest, separate and different from other days. Shabbat begins on Friday evening. Just before the sun sets the mother of the household lights two candles to welcome Shabbat. She says a blessing: 'Blessed are You O Lord our God, Ruler of the universe, Who has made us holy by your commandments and has commanded us to light the Shabbat candles.' She will have worked hard all day preparing food, as once Shabbat begins work must stop (A). The father and older sons may go to the synagogue on the Friday evening. When they return the family gathers for a special meal (B).

For Shabbat the best china and table cloth are laid and two loaves of fine bread called **hallah** (plural **hallot**) are put on the table. At the beginning of the meal the father blesses each of his children. A special song of thanks is sung in praise of the mother. It is called 'A Woman of Worth' and is from the book of *Proverbs*. Then the father recites or sings **Kiddush**. This is the blessing over the wine and everyone sips the sweet Shabbat wine. At this point the family wash their hands. Then a blessing is said over the hallot, God is thanked and everyone receives a piece of the first slice which is sprinkled with or dipped in a little salt. Hallah is pale and yellow, made with fine flour and eggs. It smells and tastes sweeter than everyday bread. In the same way Shabbat is sweeter than any other day. Quarrels are forgiven and forgotten. Shabbat is a day of peace.

At Shabbat the family may go to the synagogue on the Saturday morning. After the service everyone wishes their friends and neighbours 'Shabbat Shalom', which means a peaceful Sabbath. For 24 hours no work is done. Food has all been prepared in advance. It is a time for the family to be together. It is also

13
Shabbat

a time dedicated to God and some families read the Torah and share their thoughts on its teachings. Traditionally it has been a custom to invite a guest for Shabbat. It could be a friend or relative or a stranger who is far from their own home or family.

Shabbat ends when three faint stars can be seen in the sky on the Saturday evening. At the close of Shabbat a prayer called **Havdalah** is said. The Havdalah separates Shabbat from the new week. When the Havdalah is said a long plaited or twisted candle is lit (C). At the same time a little box of sweet spices is lifted up and passed around the family for everyone to smell the last sweetness of Shabbat. The father takes a sip of sweet wine and Shabbat is drawn to a close. Everyone hopes that its sweetness will last through the week ahead.

C *The Havdalah candle and spice box*

THINGS TO DO

1. Draw the Shabbat table. The hallah reminds Jews of the **manna** or food from heaven (*Exodus* chapter 16) when they were in the wilderness. The bread has a cloth over it to keep it from being 'shamed' as it is the last item on the table to receive a blessing. The cloth is also said to represent the dew which fell on the manna. There are two candles, reminders of the two commandments about Shabbat in the Torah. Label and explain your drawing.

2. Look up *Genesis* chapter 1 to chapter 2 verse 3, *Exodus* chapter 20 verses 8–11, *Deuteronomy* chapter 5 verse 12 and *Leviticus* chapter 23 verse 3. What do these tell us about Shabbat? What is meant by 'keep it holy'? In what ways do Jews keep Shabbat holy? Should we keep one day of the week different from others? Suggest reasons for a day of rest. Discuss these points.

3. The spice box is often ornate and shaped like a tower. Long ago spices were very rare and were kept locked away in a tower. Draw the spice box and candle. Explain the ceremony in which these are used as if you were a Jewish school pupil bringing them in to show your class.

4. Every Jewish household celebrates Shabbat in its own way. It is sometimes difficult for an RE teacher to describe what happens in the Jewish home at Shabbat because it might be different from what Jews in the class do in their homes. How can the teacher get round these problems? In what other cases will the teacher find the same sort of difficulties?

5. If you were to invite a member of a Jewish family to speak to the class about Shabbat in their home, what would you want to ask? Write a set of questions and discuss them in class.

6. There have been many discussions about what might be considered 'work' on Shabbat. What would you call work? Make a list of things which you think would certainly *not* make Shabbat a day of rest. Find out more about those things which are not permitted on Shabbat.

14
The synagogue

The synagogue is a Jewish centre for learning, meeting and prayer. In the **Tenakh** we can read about a time when the Jews were settled in Israel, once the land of Canaan. They lived through times of prosperity and difficulty but they had a homeland and a temple at Jerusalem. The temple was destroyed in 586 BCE and many Jews were forced into exile. They tried to meet in groups to hear the scriptures and worship together. Places where they met became known as synagogues or 'meeting places'. Even when the temple was rebuilt these gathering places remained centres for local worship. In 70 CE the temple was again destroyed. All the daily offerings of grain, oil and incense stopped. From then on it was the synagogue which became the focal point of worship for each Jewish community.

Every synagogue has a main hall where the congregation gathers for worship (A and B). The reading of the Torah is an important occasion and so the platform from where the Torah is read is at the centre of the synagogue. It is called the **bimah**. The **Ark** or **Aron Hakodesh** where the Torah is kept is set in the wall on the side facing Jerusalem. It is a large cupboard which is usually decorated and has an embroidered curtain. Above the Ark there are often two stone tablets representing the commandments given to Moses. On the walls either side are two prayers, one for the State of Israel and the other in English which is for the Queen and Royal Family. The seats for the congregation face the bimah and Ark. In **Orthodox** synagogues the seating for women is separate, often in a gallery upstairs. This follows the arrangements for worship which were established at the temple. There are seats for the wardens of the synagogue just next to the bimah. In front of the Ark, is a small lamp which is kept burning as a reminder of the eternal lamp of the temple in Jerusalem. Another reminder is the seven-branched candlestick, the **menorah**. There are often stained glass windows but they never depict people. This is to avoid creating images or

A *Interior of a Reform synagogue*

14
The synagogue

B *Interior of an Orthodox synagogue showing the Ark and bimah*

idols. Some synagogues are more ornate than others but most of them follow much the same general design.

There are usually classrooms for Hebrew lessons and a reception room for social gatherings. Some synagogues used to have a bakery. The synagogue has a history of being the focal point of the Jewish community. This is still true today. Some festivals are celebrated at the synagogue and of course family occasions such as births, weddings and funerals are marked by services.

THINGS TO DO

1. Draw and label a diagram of a synagogue. Use the text and photos to help you.

2. Look carefully at the two photos in this unit. Make a list of differences and similarities between the two buildings. Compare your findings with a friend. Discuss the similarities and the differences between the **Orthodox** and **Reform** synagogue in class. Find out more about Orthodox and Reform Judaism.

3. Arrange a class visit to a synagogue. If there is not one in your area make a 'model' synagogue in your classroom by rearranging the desks and improvising with objects for the Ark, and bimah etc. Do a guided tour of your synagogue.

4. In a place of worship there are often sacred objects or symbols. In the synagogue the Torah is regarded as sacred. What clues are there to show this in the synagogue? Explain your answer in a few sentences.

5. Many Jewish children go the synagogue at the weekend to learn Hebrew. Older girls and boys help the younger ones learn about the faith. Imagine you are answering questions younger children are asking about the synagogue and everything in it. Write out a sequence of questions and answers like a play.

6. Several reasons are given for women sitting separately in the synagogue. Can you suggest any? Many people's attitudes have changed concerning women in worship, women preachers and religious leaders. Some Reform synagogues now have women rabbis. Why do you think things have changed? Discuss this in class.

15
Prayer and worship

Jews can pray and worship God anywhere. Many Jews attend the synagogue at Shabbat (A). The main services are Friday night and Saturday morning but larger synagogues and especially Orthodox ones have services every day. For all synagogue worship there must be ten male Jews over the age of 13 present.

Synagogue worship is an act of praise to God. Psalms and words of adoration are recited and prayers are said. The Torah is read on four occasions during the week. The worship then involves a procession of the Sefer Torah. The Torah is not only the holy book of Judaism, it is also a symbol of God's love, his word and his promise. So it is with joy and celebration that the Torah is read. As the Torah is lifted out of the Ark a special prayer and blessing is said. The brightness of the silver crown and breastplate and the sound of the bells draw attention to the preciousness of the Torah. Everyone leans to touch the mantle of the scroll before it is carried onto the bimah. The scroll is laid on the reading desk and the bells, crown, breastplate and mantle are removed. The scroll is then unwound and the text is chanted in Hebrew. For each week of the year there are set readings. Before the scroll is returned to the Ark it is held up high for everyone to see.

The **Shema** is the declaration of the Jewish belief in the oneness of God and his relationship with Israel. It is recited as a prayer at most services (B). The **Aleynu** prayer at the close of the service speaks of the brotherhood of man and the unity of God. It also looks forward to the coming of the **Messiah** when there will be peace in the world. Prayers from the Talmud are recited and there is a prayer for the state of Israel and one prayer that is always in English, the prayer for the Queen and Royal Family.

It is not necessarily the **rabbi** who takes the service. The **hazzan** or **cantor** who is able to chant the notes correctly leads the prayers. There are prayer books in Hebrew, with a translation for non-Hebrew speakers to follow the service. Many Reform synagogues now have part of the service in the language of the community. Orthodox synagogues have kept the service in Hebrew. The atmosphere at the synagogue service is friendly and relaxed. People meet socially after the service.

A   *A Shabbat service at the synagogue*

15
Prayer and worship

In the home there are formal and informal prayers. The adult males should pray three times each day. Acts of devotion are like prayers. The Jewish mother's preparation for the Shabbat evening meal is an act of love and in a sense an act of worship. Blessings can be said on any occasion, for example over the new fruit of the season, at meal times, when smelling sweet flowers or on arriving home safely. In this way the ordinary things in life become occasions for worship.

THINGS TO DO

1. Jewish men wear a head covering such as the yamulkah for prayer. They also wear the tallit. Time set aside for God is marked out by visible signs. When we go out or meet someone important we may dress up. What does it show when we do this? What do you think it means when religious people wear special clothes for worship? Discuss these questions in class.

2. The Talmud suggests one should say 100 blessings a day. Make a list of all the things for which you could be grateful during 24 hours. Can you make it up to 100? Share your ideas.

3. The Torah is a symbol of God's love and faithfulness. Design your own symbol to represent love and faithfulness.

4. One prayer said at the synagogue is the **Amidah** or standing prayer. The last verse begins: 'Grant peace, well-being, blessing, grace loving kindness and compassion to us and to all Israel your people.' If you were a believer, what would you ask God to grant you? Would it be things or qualities of character? Write your own prayer asking God for six things.

5. Imagine you have been to the synagogue with your family. Write about what happened in the service in a paragraph or two.

6. The Holy Scriptures of Judaism speak of the coming of a king called the **Messiah**. They say he will bring in a new age of peace. Find out about the prophecies of the Messiah in the Tenakh. Look up *Isaiah* chapter 9 verses 6–7 and chapter 42 verses 1–9. What sort of hopes are expressed here? Discuss this in class.

B *Jewish men wearing prayer shawls in the synagogue*

16 Standing firm

In any faith there are those who take their commitment very seriously and those who simply follow the religious traditions of their family and whose faith has never really been tested. Many of the stories in the Jewish tradition are about people whose faith in God was tested in times of trouble but who stood firm.

At the festival of **Purim** Jews remember the story of Esther. Esther lived in Persia where many Jews were in exile. She was brought up by her uncle Mordecai who was a devout and faithful Jew. The King of Persia fell in love with Esther and they married but Esther did not tell him she was Jewish. The king had an official called Haman who was eaten up with hatred and bitterness. He despised Mordecai because he would not bow to him. Haman contrived to persuade the king that all Jews should be exterminated. When Esther heard of the plot she was horrified and frightened. Despite the risk to her own safety she disclosed to the king that she was Jewish and how she feared for her people. The king was deeply shocked when he realized the evil of the plot. He put an end to it and had Haman executed. Since then the day Esther saved her people has been a day for celebration.

At Purim this story is told in the synagogue (A). It is read from a special scroll called the **Megillah**. Children are involved in the telling of the story (B). Every time Haman's name is said it is traditional to make as much hubbub as possible. Rattles, tins full of nails, anything that makes a noise is sounded at the mention of the villain's name.

The festival of Purim is not one of the great festivals such as **Pesach, Yom Kippur** or **Rosh Hashanah**. However, its message is important. It reminds Jews of the need to stand firm in their faith even in times of difficulty. The faithfulness of Mordecai and the courage and self-sacrifice of Esther are reminders of the qualities God expects of his people. Esther and Mordecai were Jews living in exile. They were

A *Purim celebrations at the synagogue*

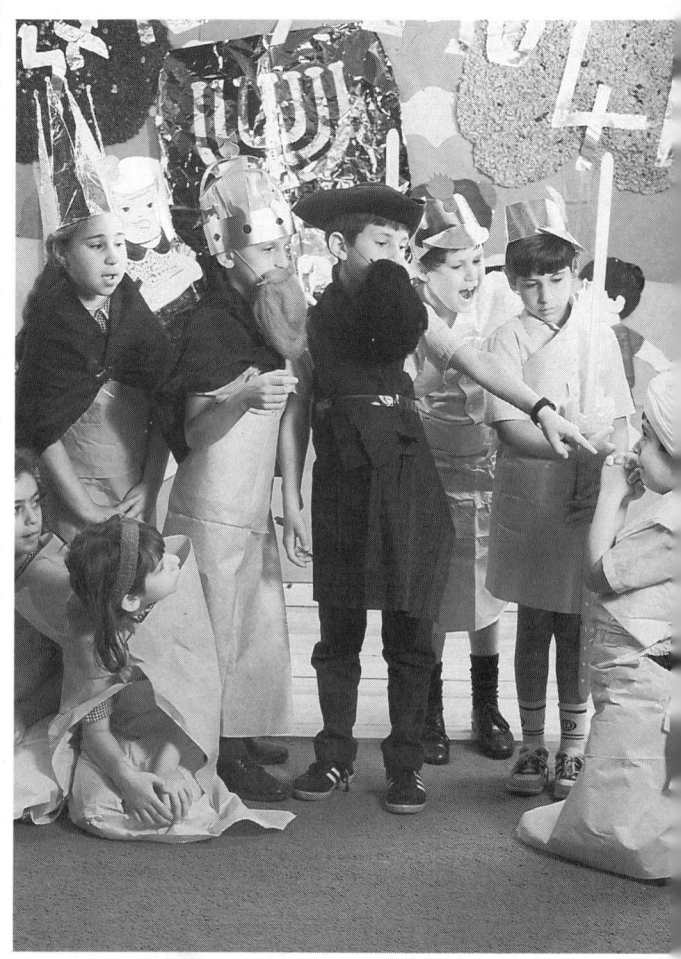

B *Purim celebrations at a Jewish school*

16
Standing firm

C *Old and new Jerusalem*

far from their homeland. It was a time when they might have slipped from their faith.

Jews living in Britain today still look to Israel as their spiritual homeland although their families may have lived in Britain for generations. There is a danger that they will lose touch with their faith if they do not keep the teachings, stories and traditions alive and pass them on to their children. Most Jews look forward to visiting Israel (C). It is an opportunity to refresh their faith and feel in touch with the traditions and history of their religion.

Celebrating festivals, listening to the stories of the scriptures and worshipping together are also ways of keeping the faith alive and binding the community together. Children are involved in the festivals as much as possible so that they too know the stories and learn a reverence for God and pass these on in turn to their own children.

THINGS TO DO

1. Look up the story of Esther in a Bible. Write up a class version of the story to act out. Make sure the audience is equipped with rattles for when the villain enters the scene.

2. Imagine you are a Jewish child preparing to go to the synagogue service at Purim. Describe what you are going to take with you and explain why you are looking forward to this occasion. Use the photo to help you.

3. It is customary at Purim to bake and eat **Hamantaschen** or pastry pockets.

   The pastry:
   300g (5 oz) margarine
   300g (5 oz) sugar
   1 egg
   250g (4 oz) self raising flour
   250g (4 oz) plain flour
   Cream the fat and sugar, add the yolk and a little of the white of egg and add the flour slowly to make a dough. Knead it lightly, roll out and cut into 24 $7\frac{1}{2}$cm (3 in) rounds.

   Filling:
   250g (4 oz) ground poppy seeds
   grated lemon rind
   150ml ($\frac{1}{4}$ pint) water
   125g (2 oz) sugar
   65g (1 oz) margarine
   65g (1 oz) sultanas
   Simmer all ingredients together until the mixture is thick. Place the cold filling in the centre of each pastry round. Brush the edges with water and bring them together to the centre to form triangles. Bake at 220°C (425°F), Mark 7 for 20 minutes. Ice them and sprinkle with coloured strands.

4. When the State of Israel was established in 1948 the news was received with great joy by Jews after the horrors of the war and Nazi Germany. Palestinians living in the area felt differently about the arrival of the newcomers. The situation today is still difficult. Find out what Israel means for Jews. Invite a Jewish person to come and speak to you about it.

5. Design a poster encouraging local Jewish children to take part in the festival of Purim at the synagogue.

6. The story of Esther is a story of religious persecution. There are many in our own society who feel persecuted because their religion and culture are not the same as the majority's. Write a story with the title 'Persecution' to give a modern example of this theme. Share your stories in class.

17

Gotama Buddha

There are some things in life which are certain. One is that we shall all die. Many people have asked how can we enjoy life when we know it is all going to come to an end? It is not possible to keep the fact of death from people. We hear about it daily on the news. We know too there is illness and suffering. We know that people grow old and die. How can we really find meaning and happiness in life if this is all we have to look forward to? These thoughts and questions were asked over 2000 years ago by someone called **Siddattha Gotama**. He later became known as the **Buddha** which means 'Enlightened One'.

The story of Gotama Buddha is dearly loved by all Buddhists. Siddattha Gotama was born in a palace in the foothills of the Himalayas. His family belonged to the princely caste and followed the ancient Vedic religion of India. His mother had a strange dream before the birth of her son. She dreamt that a white elephant had entered her side. White elephants are extremely rare. She felt this was a sign that the child would be unusual. It is said that the birth was miraculous and caused her no pain at all. A wise man predicted that the boy would be a great and powerful ruler. However, if he were once to see suffering he would become a wise and revered holy man.

Gotama's father did not want his son to become a holy man who would give up everything to live in the forest. So he took good care to see that Gotama never saw or heard of any suffering. Gotama grew up in his father's palaces. He married and had a child of his own. Despite the fact that there was nothing wrong in his life, Gotama was haunted by a feeling of restlessness. One day he persuaded his charioteer to take him out (A). The things Gotama saw outside the palace were to change his life. He saw an elderly and decrepit man. He saw a sick person in pain. He saw a corpse on

A *Buddha leaving home*

the way to cremation. Then he saw a holy man who had given up all he owned. He had a special look about him that other people did not have.

Gotama gave up his life in the palace (B). He left his wife and child and exchanged his fine clothes for the rags of a wandering holy man. In the hope of overcoming suffering he joined the much respected forest dwellers, holy men who gave up everything to devote their lives to the search for the Truth. Gotama practised the hardest **meditation** exercises and fasted almost to the point of death. However, he felt this was pointless. He broke his fast and ate a small meal of rice. His friends left him in disgust. Gotama seated himself under a sacred **Bodhi** tree to **meditate**. He resolved not to move until he reached the Truth. Under the Bodhi tree Gotama gained **enlightenment**. He became free from the fires of greed, hatred and ignorance. He was no longer burning with desires of selfishness and fears of suffering and death. He found the peace of **Nibbana**. Nibbana means 'blown out' like a flame, it is often described as a state of bliss or liberation.

17
Gotama Buddha

B *The Buddha*

THINGS TO DO

1. Photo A shows an illustrated page from a manuscript telling the story of the Buddha leaving the palace. Tell the story of the Buddha in your own words and pictures.

2. Gotama was kept free from all evidence of suffering. Would it be possible to do this today? It is quite natural for parents to want to shield their young children from the terrible things in the world. Do you think this is a good idea? Would you do the same for your child? Discuss these questions in class.

3. The birth stories of great religious leaders often tell of signs and miracles. Why do you think this is? What other birth stories do you know? Compare two and discuss the similarities and differences in class.

4. If you had everything you wanted and knew nothing of pain or death would you be happy? How would it feel to be in this situation? Write a description of how you would feel, what questions you would ask and how you would react to such a life. Write it in poetry or prose.

5. Is it possible to be completely happy knowing that life eventually ends in death? Discuss this question in groups. Share your ideas in class. Make a class survey of responses.

6. What do you think was the effect of seeing old age, sickness and death on the Buddha? Design a Buddhist poster which represents these three things.

18 The Middle Path

After gaining enlightenment Gotama felt compassion for all beings caught up in the suffering of existence. He decided to devote the rest of his life to serving others and teaching them the way to Nibbana (A). The word Buddha means 'Awakened One'. The Buddha saw that most people lived their lives 'unawakened'. They did not see things as they really are but went about their lives as if asleep. The teachings of the Buddha are intended to wake people up to the truth. The teachings are summed up in the **Four Noble Truths** and the **Middle Path**.

The Four Noble Truths are:

1 Life is unsatisfactory and full of suffering. This means we can never really be happy. When we cannot get what we want we are unhappy and when we have what we want we are anxious that it will not last. So there is no long term contentment.

2 We suffer in this way because we are always wanting. We cannot help craving for things. Craving is due to greed, hatred and ignorance.

3 The answer to the problem is to stop the craving. This is very hard.

4 The way to stop the craving is to follow a 'Middle Path'. This way does not lead to self indulgence neither does it mean giving up everything and depriving oneself. It is between these two extremes.

The Middle Path begins with:
1 **Right Understanding** and
2 **Right Thought.**

Awakening to the Truth means seeing things as they really are. According to the Buddha this means understanding that wanting only leads to making ourselves and others unhappy. Understanding the Four Noble Truths is the way to Right Understanding. Right Thought is thinking which is free from evil, free from greed, envy, hatred and unkindness.

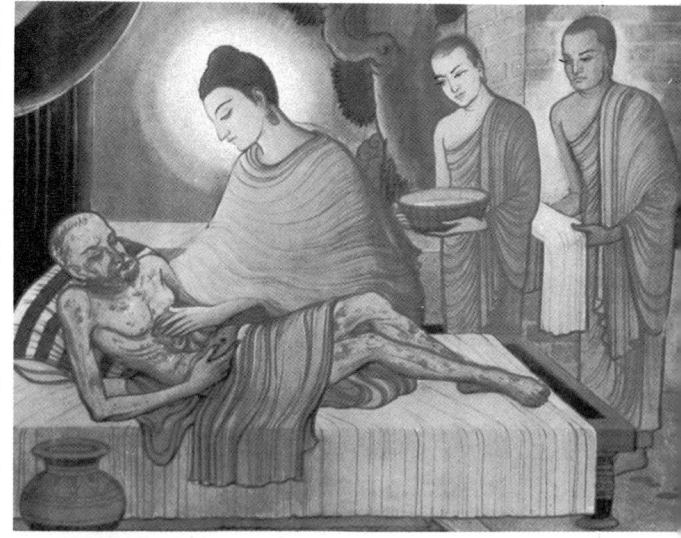

A *Buddha*

B *The Buddhist wheel of eternal rebirth*

18
The Middle Path

The next three points of the Middle Path are:
3 **Right Speech**,
4 **Right Action** and
5 **Right Livelihood**.

These are all essential to a life which is unselfish and does not harm others.

The last three concerns of the Middle Path are:
6 **Right Effort**,
7 **Right Mindfulness** and
8 **Right Concentration**.

The Middle Path is not easy. It demands perseverence in overcoming greed, hatred and ignorance. It means being very clear about ones intentions in life and not just muddling through. It means being aware and awake. Right Concentration is achieved through meditation and self discipline.

These teachings of the Buddha are called the **Dhamma** or **Truth**. Gotama Buddha taught the Dhamma to his first followers at Benares (C). He sent them out with the words: 'Go now and wander out of compassion for the world, for the benefit, welfare and happiness of gods and men. Teach the Dhamma.'

C *Buddha the teacher*

THINGS TO DO

1 The Dhamma says life is unsatisfactory and full of suffering. Is there any truth in this? Is there long term happiness? List 10 things which prevent you from being really happy. Add to your list 10 things which cause people in the world to suffer. Compare ideas and discuss whether the First Noble Truth is true.

2 In the Buddhist wheel of eternal rebirth (Illustration B) the pig, the snake and the cockerel stand for greed, hatred and ignorance. These three things tie the beings of the world to endless rebirth. How would you represent these evils? Draw symbols for them.

3 According to the Dhamma all suffering is due to wanting. For example, if we want something and we don't get it we are unhappy. Is all suffering due to wanting? What part do the evils of greed, hatred and ignorance play? Think of three examples of suffering in the world. In pairs, discuss the causes behind each example. Assess the truth of the Buddha's teaching.

4 What are Right Speech, Right Action and Right Livelihood? It might be easier to think of their opposites. Make three sets of two columns with the headings:
(a) **Right Speech – Wrong Speech**
(b) **Right Action – Wrong Action**
(c) **Right Livelihood – Wrong Livelihood**
Write examples under each heading.

5 Do people muddle through life without any real direction or intention? How do people try to find happiness in their lives? Draw a cartoon strip to illustrate *one* of the following:
● A path to happiness which does not last.
● A path to happiness that lasts.

6 The Buddha speaks of gods and men. Some Buddhists accept the existence of beings such as spirits and gods. Like humans they believe they are born and die and are reborn. Do you believe in supernatural beings? What sort of existence do you think they have? What part do they play in the world? Discuss these questions in class.

19

Monks, nuns and lay people

The first disciples of the Buddha followed his example. They gave up the usual pattern of work, home and family to become wandering monks, meditating and teaching the Dhamma. This was how Buddhism first began. The Buddha's following grew and spread through India between 500 BCE and 1000 CE. It developed in two main ways. These ways became known as **Theravada** and **Mahayana** Buddhism. Theravada Buddhism moved into South East Asia and is now found in places such as Burma, Sri Lanka and Thailand. Mahayana developed later and went into Central Asia, China, Mongolia, Korea, Vietnam, Japan and Tibet.

Theravada means 'The way of the Elders'. This way goes back to very early Buddhism. Many Theravada Buddhists today still devote their lives to the quest for Nibbana. They give up the normal pattern of home, family and work and join a community of monks and nuns.

Theravada monks and nuns are known as **bhikkhus** and **bhikkhunis** meaning 'those who receive **alms**'. This is because they rely on the lay community for gifts of food and provisions. The community of monks and nuns is called the **Sangha**. The day of the Sangha begins before dawn with meditation and religious chants. Breakfast is small and simple. The main meal is at noon after which all monks and nuns fast. Time is spent studying the teachings of the Buddha, practising meditation, offering devotion at the shrine of the Buddha and listening to the sermons of the senior monks.

Like all Buddhists monks and nuns express their intentions for life by repeating three times the **Three Jewels**: 'I take refuge in the Buddha, I take refuge in the Dhamma and I take refuge in the Sangha.' Monks and nuns entering the Sangha keep the **Ten Precepts**. Some of these are kept by all Buddhists. The Ten Precepts are:

1. To refrain from killing or injuring living creatures
2. To refrain from taking what is not given
3. To refrain from any sexual activity
4. To refrain from lying and wrong speech
5. To refrain from intoxicants
6. To refrain from eating after midday
7. To refrain from entertainments
8. To avoid use of ornaments and perfumes
9. To refrain from sleeping in a luxury bed
10. To avoid handling money.

A *Three Buddhist monks in Saffron robes, with shaven heads and alms bowls*

19

Monks, nuns and lay people

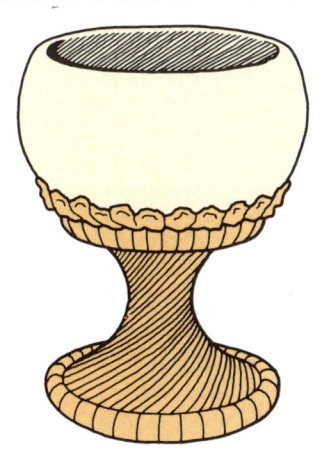

B *An alms bowl and holder*

Fully ordained monks keep a stricter code and own nothing but a bowl, their saffron robes and a razor to shave (A and B). Monks and nuns shave all the hair on their heads as a sign of living simply and giving up self pride.

The Sangha serves an important function in the lay community. Lay Buddhists are not monks or nuns. They try to follow the Dhamma in their everyday lives at work and in the home (C). The lay community treasures the Sangha in their midst. It is a beacon keeping alight the example of the Buddha. Every morning the bhikkhus walk out into the community with their alms bowls to collect food for the day. The local people consider it a privilege to provide for the monks. In return the Sangha is there for people to hear the teachings of the Buddha.

THINGS TO DO

1. Draw the Sri Lankan Buddhist monk with his yellow robe, his shaven head and alms bowl. Write a magazine article about the type of life these things represent. You could interview the monk for your article.

2. Look again at the Ten Precepts. If you were to keep numbers 1, 2, 6 and 7 what would you have to give up? Describe the changes in your life that would have to be made.

3. What do you understand by the words 'to take refuge'. Why do you think the Three Refuges are called the Three Jewels? What things do people normally take refuge in in our society? Discuss these points in class. Design a card or poster to represent the Three Jewels.

4. The Sangha provides an opportunity for people to hear the Buddha's teachings, learn meditation and join in the life of the monks and nuns. In return the community serves the Sangha. Represent this two-way support and enrichment in a diagram with pictures.

5. Some people argue that Buddhism is a selfish religion concerned only with gaining personal enlightenment. What evidence is there to contradict this? Are all religions open to this criticism? Write your answers and discuss them in class.

6. An alms bowl must be cared for. This encourages awareness or **mindfulness**. The Buddha gave his monks and nuns guidelines:
   - Each bowl must have a cover to protect it and make it easier to carry.
   - It is not to be put on the ground without protection nor left where it could fall.
   - Hard or sharp objects should not be used to scrape it.
   - It should not be held without support and should be washed and dried with great care.

   Draw the alms bowl. Describe its purpose and how it should be cared for.

C *Lay Buddhists at a monastery*

20
The shrine

A The shrine room: the monk is performing puja

The life of the Sangha is not suited to everyone; most people are busy with work and bringing up a family. They may try to follow the Buddha and his Path in their daily lives and express their devotion at a **shrine**.

At the Sangha monks, nuns and lay people attend devotion at the shrine (A). People remove their shoes when they enter the shrine room. This is to leave the dirt outside and it is a sign of respect. An image of the Buddha provides a focus for meditation. The beauty, peace and serenity shown in the image lend an atmosphere of calm. People enter quietly and, with their hands together, bow before the Buddha image. They might stand before the shrine and touch their forehead, mouth and chest with their hands together. The mind, speech and body are offering devotion. The shrine is the focus for meditation as well as devotional offerings. People sit quietly contemplating the image or meditating (B).

B Lay Buddhists at the monastery

20
The shrine

In the Theravada tradition, full moon and new moon and the mid points between, are times when monks and nuns have to reflect on their failures and confess their moments of weakness or unkindness. These are called **Uposatha** days in Buddhist countries. Most people do not go to work on Uposatha days and they make a point of not eating any meat. Families get together to provide a meal for the Sangha. Some spend the whole day there visiting the shrine and listening to sermons.

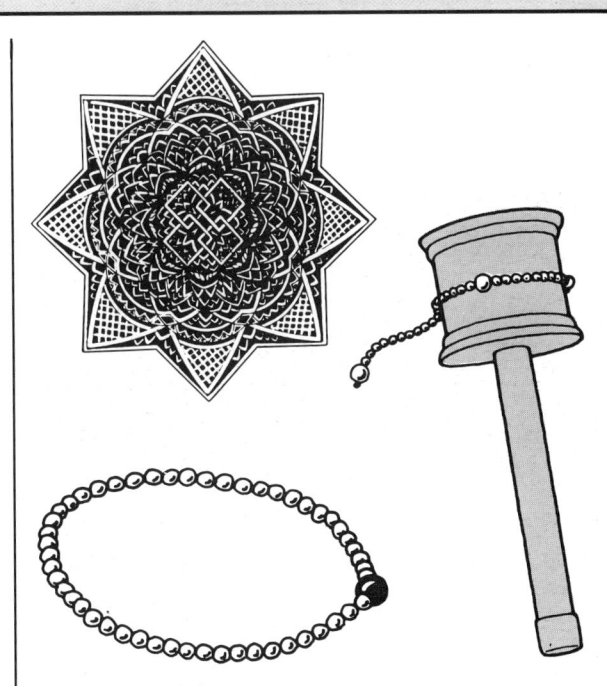

C *Mala, mandala and prayer wheel*

Some Buddhists find it helpful to repeat the words of a **mantra**. A mantra is like a simple prayer or blessing. A **mala** or prayer beads may be used to keep count of the times the mantra is repeated (C). In the Sangha the monks present the ritual offerings. These are usually flowers, light and incense. These acts of devotion are called **puja**. The people watch and listen to the prayers:

> In reverence to the Buddha we offer incense
> Incense whose fragrance fills the air
> The fragrance of the perfect life, sweeter than incense
> Spreads in all directions throughout the world.

Most Buddhists have a shrine at home with a small Buddha image on a shelf. It is kept in the highest room or on the highest shelf. Offerings are made daily and incense and light are burnt before the image.

Some lay Buddhists practise meditation. Through meditation the Buddhist becomes 'mindful' so their thoughts and actions are governed by loving kindness rather than selfishness. To be 'mindful' the mind must be calm, not constantly distracted and out of control. Some Buddhists use a mandala to focus on in meditation. For most Buddhists daily meditation serves to calm and control the mind but the ultimate aim of meditation is to reach **Nibbana**.

THINGS TO DO

1. Read the prayer for the offering of incense. Write another prayer Buddhists might say when offering light or flowers.

2. Imagine you are a Buddhist. Your family and others are providing a meal for the Sangha. Write your plan of things to remember and describe your preparations and excitement.

3. Monastic life is not for everyone. Why do you think that most people are *not* involved in such a way of life? Discuss.

4. Draw the shrine, using Photo A to help you. Imagine you are a monk or nun explaining the things in the shrine room to visitors. Write your explanation under your drawing.

5. Some Buddhists use a mala. In Tibet they use a **prayer wheel** which contains a written mantra. Turning the wheel is like saying the mantra. Draw the mala, wheel and the mandala and explain their uses.

6. Meditation begins with stilling the mind. Try to do this. Sit comfortably, not slouching. Relax and be calm. Close your eyes or look downwards. Rest your hands in your lap or on your knees. Breathe regularly and gently. Concentrate on the air entering and leaving your body as you breathe. Try to keep your thoughts on this, when distractions come to mind let them go; don't hang on to them and don't try to fight them off. Just let them pass through and go on their way and return your thoughts to your breathing, counting if necessary. Spend a couple of minutes on this. Then break and discuss the difficulties you had with a friend. Then try again for a longer span of time.

21 Buddhism in Britain

Many of the Buddhists in Britain are following in the traditions of their religious and cultural background. They are from families originating from Sri Lanka, Thailand, Burma and Vietnam. There are also many people who have chosen the path of Buddhism but who were not born into a traditional Buddhist family or culture (A). There are several **Theravada** monastic communities in this country. The majority of the monks and nuns are not from Buddhist families. The communities nevertheless have the friendship and support of the Thai, Burmese and Sri Lankan families here in Britain. The Sangha are run on traditional lines. Bhikkhus wear saffron robes and collect alms in the neighbourhood. People also bring food to the Sangha. This is an important occasion as it binds the relationship between the Sangha and the lay community.

The room where the meal is eaten is set out with a place prepared for each nun and monk.

A   *A Buddhist monastery in Britain*

This is a clean space to sit cross-legged on the floor, with a jug of water for drinking and washing. The order for seating depends on the length of time a monk has been ordained. The people who bring food take off their shoes before entering the room. The monks and nuns receive their food in silence, without asking for anything. There is a special atmosphere in the room as the people give the food. Giving alms is an act of loving kindness. It brings blessing to those who give as well as those who receive (B). Before they eat, the monks recite a traditional blessing. Those who have brought the food listen quietly and thoughtfully.

B   *Monks receiving food*

There are often visitors to the Sangha. They come to hear the teachings of the Buddha, to meditate and to join in the life of the community. Some Theravada communities in Britain now offer classes for children. The Sangha is a symbol in the community keeping alight the way of loving kindness and compassion and standing for wisdom and peace in the world.

The **Mahayana** schools in Britain have also adapted to serve people in the West and to help them on the road to enlightenment. They have centres for learning and offer courses on meditation. They do not have an alms round but they do rely on voluntary support for funds. In Mahayana Buddhism the Sangha is important but other paths to enlightenment are offered. It is believed that there are many enlightened beings or Buddhas. A Buddha is born on earth only once in 1000 years or so but there are Buddhas in other realms of the universe. These beings can help people on the path to enlightenment. An essential concept in Mahayana Buddhism is the belief in the work of **Bodhisattas** (C). A Bodhisatta is an enlightened being who does not take on the bliss of **Nirvana** (Nibbana) but returns over and over to the world to help other beings become free from suffering. The Bodhisatta is an example of loving kindness and perfect compassion. (Nirvana is Sanskrit for the Pali Nibbana, Bodhisattva is Sanskrit for the Pali Bodhisatta. Mahayana use Sanskrit and Theravada use Pali.)

21
Buddhism in Britain

THINGS TO DO

1 When the first Buddhist communities were set up in Britain some people were suspicious, some were tolerant, others were welcoming. Imagine a Buddhist Sangha is to be set up in your neighbourhood. Write a newspaper article discussing the hopes and fears of the neighbours and the hopes of the Buddhists.

2 The best known Bodhisatta is **Avalokiteshvara** (Photo C) honoured in the Mahayana schools of Tibet, Japan and China. His outstretched hand is a symbol of compassion. Draw your own symbol of loving kindness and compassion. Explain its meaning.

3 Buddhists believe that all beings have 'Buddha nature' but it is hidden, like the moon behind clouds. Is there something eternal and perfect in us? What would you call this? How do we know it is there? Do you think there is the potential for enlightenment in everyone? Discuss these questions.

4 Find out more about Buddhist communities in Britain. Write to the Amaravati Buddhist Centre, Gt Gaddesden, Hemel Hempstead, Herts HP1 3BZ or The Madhyamaka Centre, Kilnwick Percy Hall, Pocklington, York to find out what they do.

5 Those who give alms say it gives them a special feeling inside when they stand before the line of silent monks and nuns who humbly receive without asking. Imagine offering food you have prepared. How would you feel? What would it be like? Discuss this and write a story or a poem called 'Giving'.

6 When they see the bhikkhus with their alms bowls, some people make fun of them, others stand and stare, some may ask them what they are doing. Buddhists feel it is important that they are seen and that people find out about them and their way of life. Act out a short play in which people respond differently to the presence of bhikkhus with their alms bowls in the street. Show how you would expect the bhikkhu to respond too.

C *Avalokiteshvara, the best known Bodhisatta*

22

The way things are

A *Buddhist monks study the scriptures*

The most important word for all Buddhists is **Dhamma**. This word can be translated in many ways. It could be said to mean 'the Truth about the way things are'. It might be interpreted as 'Law' or 'what is Right'. It could also be translated as 'Teaching' or the 'Word of the Buddha'. Dhamma is contained in the teaching of the Buddha. For Buddhists it is the Truth. However, the Buddha said no one should just accept his teaching. Each person must test it for themselves in their own experience.

The teaching of the Buddha was treasured by his first followers. After his death they recited his teachings and memorized them. The words were handed down in different dialects and languages. The most complete collection of these teachings is in the language of Pali. The **Pali texts** are the scriptures of the Theravada (A). They are called the **Tipitaka** or 'the three baskets'. The Tipitaka contains the sayings of the Buddha, his rules of discipline for bhikkhus, and philosophical discussion on teachings.

Mahayana Buddhists have their own texts in Sanskrit, Chinese, Tibetan and Japanese as well as Pali. They make up a treasure house of stories, teachings and ideas to help people on the path to enlightenment. Many of the texts are the same as those of the Pali scriptures. Some are later teachings which have been handed down with the Buddha's own words. Most Buddhist Sangha have a library containing copies of the scriptures so that people can study them. Sometimes the scriptures are displayed in the shrine or meditation room. They are given a place of honour because they contain the word of the Buddha (B). The Buddha knew that people need to be taught in different ways as well as in different dialects and languages. He was quite happy for the Dhamma to be translated. Sometimes he used stories to teach so ordinary people could remember and understand. The story of Kisa Gotami shows how Dhamma is to be found in experience as well as in teachings.

22
The way things are

Kisa Gotami was the mother of a young boy. Her son became ill and died. She was beside herself with grief. Picking up the boy she went from house to house asking for medicine, but of course no one could help her. Then she met a wise man who suggested she ask the Buddha. The Buddha said he could help her. He sent her to collect three grains of mustard seed, each one from a house in which no one had ever died. As Kisa Gotami went from home to home she found out that every household had lost a loved one. Everyone had a sadness in their life. Humbled by what she had learnt, she cremated her son and returned to the Buddha to follow his teaching.

THINGS TO DO

1. The scriptures in Photo B are written on palm leaves. These are threaded together. The Buddhist scriptures are divided into **Suttas**. Sutta means thread. The stories and teachings were collected with a common thread or theme running through them. Draw the scriptures and explain what they are.

2. Bhikkhus spend part of their time studying the scriptures. You now know other details of their routine and practice. Write up the daily timetable of a monk or nun at a Theravada Sangha.

3. Buddhism teaches people to see that all things change. Nothing is permanent. Sit in a group. In the middle, light a single candle. Spend five minutes just watching the flame, then think about these questions:

- Is the flame you watched at the beginning the same flame as the one you watched at the end of the period?
- Has it changed?
- Can you tell when the change took place? Discuss these questions in your group. Make a list of the changes that have taken place in the candle, in you, in the room, outside too in the five minutes. Is anything exactly the same as when you began the exercise?

4. Read again the story of Kisa Gotami. Act it out in class and develop the stories of those who lost their loved ones. Discuss the meaning and teaching to be found in the story.

5. The **Four Noble Truths** and the **Middle Path** are at the heart of the Dhamma. Design a booklet of Buddhist teachings you know.

6. One of the teachings of Buddhism is that the idea of having an individual 'self' is misleading. It leads to claims such as 'me' and 'mine' and these lead to possessiveness, selfishness and greed. The answer is to let go of this idea of self. Buddhists are taught that the self is not real or lasting. They are taught to ask whether they have a self at all. Is there a self? Can we point to it? Is it always the same? Does it last for ever? What is it? Discuss the questions in class.

B *Buddhist scriptures written on palms*

23
Seasons and festivals

Buddhist festivals focus on the life of the Buddha or the life of the Sangha. Traditionally, Buddhist monks travelled from place to place teaching the Dhamma. In India, where Buddhism first grew up, the monsoon prevented the monks from travelling for three months of the year and they had to take shelter. This became known as the **Rains Retreat**. Originally the local community offered shelter and welcomed their visitors with a great procession. Most monks now stay in their own Sangha at this time, but the season is still a festive time when lay Buddhists visit the Sangha with gifts of food.

At the end of the rains retreat there is an important occasion called the **Kathina** ceremony. Kathina means cloth or robe, and the lay community present the monks with new saffron coloured robes. In so doing they gain merit for future lives. This is an occasion for taking festive foods to the Sangha and people stay to listen to a sermon on the teachings of the Buddha. The Kathina ceremony is a very ancient festival and is mentioned in the Buddhist scriptures.

The best known Buddhist festival is **Wesak**, also called Vesakha (A). This festival is not referred to in the scriptures. In the Theravada tradition, Wesak marks the birth, enlightenment and death of the Buddha. In some countries it is the enlightenment of the Buddha which is the focus of attention and in others such as Japan it is just the birth of the Buddha which is celebrated. The customs and traditions vary. In some communities lanterns and lamps are lit at dusk around the temples, Sanghas and shrines (B). Some Sanghas have a Bodhi tree which is a symbol of the enlightenment of the Buddha. At Wesak the tree is watered and decorated with lanterns. The lay community arrive at the monasteries, temples and shrines with offerings to put before the Buddha image and with gifts of food for the monks (C). They stay to listen to the sermons about the Dhamma. In many Buddhist lands at

A *The Buddha is a focus of Wesak celebrations*

Lanterns and candle for Wesak

Decorated night light/candle, on a plate/saucer

B *Wesak lanterns and candles*

Seasons and festivals

Wesak, sermons are broadcast over the television and radio so people can hear them at home. In Thailand lay Buddhists visit their local Sangha carrying candles, flowers and incense. They circle the shrine and **Bodhi** tree keeping them on their right as a sign of respect. Some lay Buddhists spend this special time fasting or take a vow of silence. In this way they remember the death of the Buddha as well as his enlightenment.

Festivals in Buddhist countries are sometimes marked by public holidays. There are celebrations and special foods and people visit family and friends. No meat is eaten and to avoid harming any living creature all farming stops. Some Buddhists try to make these times occasions for renewing their intention to follow the Buddha. They may spend the day at the Sangha following the routine of the monks and nuns. Buddhist communities in this country celebrate these festivals in their own ways and adapt the traditions to fit the new environment. Wesak parties are arranged for children and for adults there are opportunities to practise meditation, to hear the teachings of the Buddha and to join in the life of the Sangha.

THINGS TO DO

1. Festivals are special for most people. Buddhists feel that they are opportunities for showing 'loving kindness'. What examples of loving kindness can you find in the celebrations? Write a few sentences about them.

2. The enlightenment of the Buddha is represented in the symbol of light at Wesak. Make or draw a Wesak lantern or candle and explain its meaning.

3. The rainy season was a time for retreat. How would you spend three months on retreat? Imagine you are out in the country, you have no television or other entertainment and no money but you are provided with water, food, a library and shelter. How could you make this a valuable time? Discuss this in class.

4. Festivals help to bring the community together and encourage people to remember the religious side to life. Make a leaflet or poster for a Sangha in Britain to advertise and explain Wesak and to invite people to join in its celebrations.

5. Greetings cards are exchanged at Wesak. Design a card which shows the religious meaning of the festival.

6. In Tibet the authorities are hostile to Buddhism. At festivals emotions are often aroused. In such instances there can be clashes. Why do you think that some political powers do not tolerate religion? Why do political beliefs sometimes clash with religious beliefs? Discuss these points in class.

C   *Lay Buddhists approaching a monastery*

24
Jesus Christ

A The baptism of Jesus

Christians believe in one **God**, whose love and power can be seen in the world he created. They believe that God spoke through prophets whose words are in the **Bible**, their holy book. The central belief of the Christian faith is that God spoke to the world in a unique way in the person of **Jesus Christ**. To express this very special relationship between God and Jesus, Christians call Jesus the **Son of God**. They believe Jesus revealed God in human form.

Jesus was born into a Jewish family in about 6 CE, in Palestine. Little is known about his early life. At about the age of 30 he came into the public eye at his **baptism** (A). There was a powerful preacher at this time, called **John**. He was baptizing people with water in the river Jordan. This was a symbol of a new beginning. He told them they must ask God to forgive their sins and begin a new life because the **Messiah** was coming. The Jews were expecting a king, who would set up God's kingdom on earth. Jesus came to be baptized and John recognized him as the promised Messiah. The word Messiah is Hebrew for 'anointed' because the kings of Israel were anointed with oil. The Greek for Messiah is Christ.

Jesus became a travelling preacher with a group of 12 followers or **disciples**. He taught in the towns and villages around Galilee. Thousands came to hear him. His message was quite simple. God was waiting, like a father with open arms, ready to forgive the sins of all who turned to him, no matter what they had done. Jesus acted out this message of God's love and compassion in his own life, opening his arms to the lonely and unloved. He befriended the poor and healed the sick.

Jesus was not popular with everyone. He condemned the religious leaders of the time. They prided themselves on their own holiness but ignored the rights of the poor. They took great care to keep the religious laws and rituals but turned a blind eye to those in need. The religious authorities were jealous of Jesus' popularity and angry at the way he put them to shame. They despised him for mixing with sinners and people they saw as 'unclean'. Feeling threatened by Jesus' success they plotted his arrest and tried him under false charges. They accused him of starting a rebellion and claiming to be a king. The Roman governor, **Pontius Pilate**, could not find any evidence against him. However, he wanted to keep the peace so he gave permission for Jesus' death. Jesus died hanging on a cross. This was a cruel Roman form of execution. His body was wrapped in a shroud and buried in a tomb carved out of rock.

The disciples deserted Jesus, terrified they too might be arrested. They hid, deeply shocked and frightened. However, something happened which changed their lives. They felt the power and presence of Jesus as if he were alive and with them again. Forgetting their fears, the disciples proclaimed that Jesus was alive, he had risen and overcome death. This was the beginning of the Christian faith and is still the message of the Christian Church today.

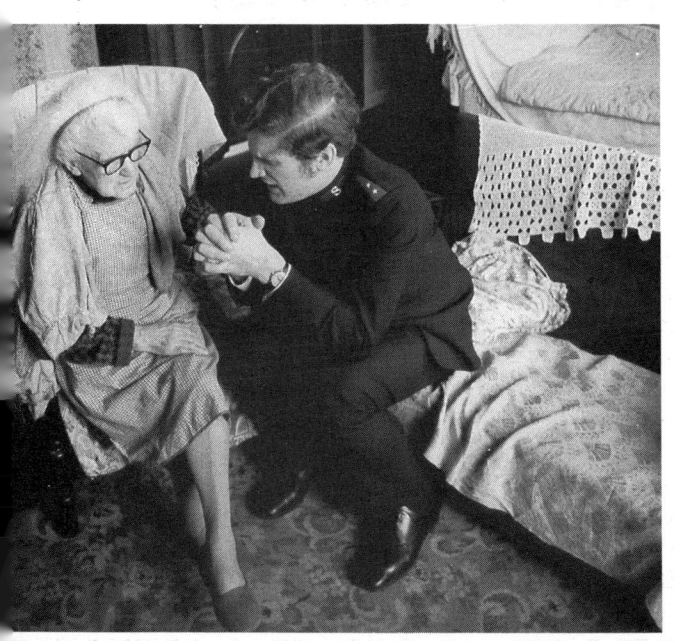

24
Jesus Christ

THINGS TO DO

1. People still say this is a Christian country. What do you think they mean? Do people follow Christ's example? What is his example? Discuss this in class.

2. Read the story of the baptism of Jesus in the Bible. One version is in Mark's Gospel, chapter 1 verses 1–11. Look at the painting of the story in Photo A. What are the writer and the painter telling us about Jesus by using symbols? Why do you think the writer chose the symbol of the dove? Tell the story in your own words, or illustrate it.

3. Jesus befriended the people who no one else wanted to know. Who are the outcast and unloved in the world today (B)? Find articles in newspapers which indicate the groups and individuals rejected or hated or simply left unnoticed and unloved in our society. Who is befriending these people today?

4. Many of the Jews were expecting a military leader, a Messiah who would overthrow the Romans and establish Israel as a powerful nation. Jesus had a different idea of God's kingdom. What do you think 'the Kingdom of God' should be like? How do you think other people imagine it? Share your ideas in class.

5. Christians call Jesus 'Risen Lord' and believe he is alive today, working through his followers. They also feel they can turn to him as a friend. This experience of the Risen Lord is central to the Christian faith. What do Christians mean by 'Jesus lives'? Invite a Christian to speak to the class about this.

6. Many of Jesus' stories are called **parables** because they draw 'parallels' and say something is like something else. One of the best loved is the Lost Son in Luke's Gospel, chapter 15 verses 11–32. Read the story. Do you think this story says anything about:
   - God
   - sinners
   - the danger of thinking you are better than other people?

   Does the story tell us anything else? Who do you think it was for? Discuss your answers.

B *The Salvation Army help the needy*

25

Bread and wine

On the night he was arrested, Jesus shared a special meal with his disciples. At the supper he broke up a piece of bread saying it was his body. He knew his own body would soon be broken on the cross. He gave the bread to the disciples to eat. It was to be a sign of his promise of love and friendship. After the meal, he poured the wine and said it was his blood. He knew his blood would soon be shed. This too would be a sign of his love for them and seal God's promise of forgiveness. Jesus gave the cup to the disciples to drink and said they should remember him every time they shared wine in this way. Christians today gather to share the bread and the cup to remember Jesus' meal of love. Churches do this in different ways.

In the **Roman Catholic** church the sharing of bread and wine is called the **Mass** (A). It is referred to as a celebration and begins with joyful words of praise to God. The worshippers listen to readings from the holy scriptures and a sermon given by the priest. Prayers are said, some are words of thanks and praise, some are for those in need. Christians prepare their minds and hearts before receiving the bread and wine. Kneeling, they remember times of weakness, selfishness or unkindness and ask God to forgive them and help them to try again. Many Catholics like to go to a priest for **confession** before taking Mass. At Mass the priest blesses and **consecrates** the **host**. The host is the wafer symbolizing the bread, it is the body of Christ. Each person receives the host. The wine, too, is consecrated and takes on the meaning of the blood of Christ. The service of bread and wine is a **sacrament** and carries spiritual blessing and meaning. When Catholics receive the host they believe they are receiving the living presence of Christ.

The **Anglican** service is very similar to the Roman Catholic Mass. It is often called the **Eucharist**, meaning 'Thanksgiving'.

A   *A Roman Catholic Mass held out of doors*

25
Bread and wine

Sometimes real bread is broken. The whole congregation shares one cup or **chalice**. As the priest gives the bread he says, 'The Body of Christ,' and as he gives the wine he says, 'The blood of Christ.' The bread and wine are sacraments and symbols of the death of Christ.

In **Baptist** and **Methodist** churches, everyone receives a separate cup (B). It contains grape juice rather than wine. The sharing of the bread and cup is an act of remembrance of the last supper and not the receiving of sacraments. Some Christian groups meet in their own homes to share the bread and wine and have no priest or minister to lead the service.

The sharing of the **Lord's Supper** is always a very special occasion. Many different emotions are expressed in the service. Feelings of joy, adoration and thanksgiving, feeling sorry and the sense of being forgiven and having a chance to make a fresh start. There is also the feeling of oneness with other Christians who share the same meal and the sense of meeting Christ through re-enacting the last supper.

B   *The Lord's Supper in a Methodist church*

THINGS TO DO

1. Read an account of the last supper in Mark's Gospel, chapter 14 verses 12–31. It says it was **Passover** that Jesus shared with his disciples. What event would have been remembered at the table that night? It would have been a special occasion and an emotional one. There are themes of love and friendship, blood and betrayal, faithfulness and failure. Represent these themes in symbols in a design for a church window.

2. Some churches have a service with bread and wine every week, or even every day, others only celebrate **Communion** once or twice a year. Find out about the ways in which the last supper is re-enacted in different churches. Make a chart or write a report explaining the differences and the reasons behind them.

3. The **Society of Friends** and **Salvation Army** do not have a Communion service. They say that every shared meal is an act of communion and should be treated as such. Why is sharing food with someone significant? On what special occasions is a meal shared? What is the difference between eating on your own and eating with others? Discuss this in class.

4. If your class were to have a friendship meal once a week with everyone bringing something, what problems would arise? How would you deal with them? What good things might come from such a meal? Early Christians met to share a meal. You can read about this in St Paul's first letter to the Corinthians, chapter 11 verses 17–34. Discuss the problems that were arising and the advice offered.

5. Most churches have services which are not the 'Lord's Supper'. A regular family service will be a time of prayer and thanksgiving with hymns and Bible readings and a sermon. Design a short service. Choose Bible readings, prayers and hymns on the theme of 'forgiveness'.

6. In the **Orthodox**, Anglican and Roman Catholic churches sharing of the bread and wine is one of the sacraments. Sacraments are more than symbols, they are holy because it is believed God works through them. Draw the bread and wine and explain their meaning in these churches.

26
Followers

A *Christians praising God*

When Jesus chose his disciples he said, 'Follow me'. Christians try to follow Jesus in their daily lives. Christian parents try to bring up their children knowing stories from Jesus' teaching and life. They encourage their children to get into the habit of praying, teaching them the words of the **Lord's prayer** which Jesus taught his disciples (A). Most Christian families attend church regularly and the children may go to Sunday school. Through pictures, hymns, prayers and stories they learn the teachings of the faith. Many Christians are involved in helping at their church, serving coffee after the service or running the creche or Sunday school. Others hold Bible study groups in their homes or provide transport to church for the elderly.

In the home the Christian family expresses the faith in their daily routine. Prayers may be said before and after meals to thank God for his goodness. Parents try to set a good example. The family may put aside time to study the Bible together or pray together each week. Most Christians read their Bible daily to find guidance and comfort from its teachings. Sometimes life gets too busy to find sufficient time for real prayer and Bible study. Many churches organize **retreats** where members of the congregation can spend a few days in thought and prayer and Bible study with other Christians. These are residential courses, usually held at a centre in the country or even at a monastery or convent. There are of course some Christians who devote their entire lives to God in this way and who join a monastic order of monks or nuns (B). Some of these communities are involved in active work in the community, teaching or serving the poor and oppressed.

B *Nuns in the grounds of their convent*

26 Followers

C *A youth club in a city church*

There are many Christians who feel that, like Jesus, they must take a stand against poverty, greed and selfishness. In Korea and Latin America many Christians identify with the struggles of the very poor. They are working for a fairer system. In South Africa there are Christians fighting for equality, justice and freedom for the black majority. In Britain, individual churches are involved in making collections for charity and are often busy in their own areas trying to serve the community. The church in Photo C is providing a place for young people to get together. Many of the black church communities in Britain are determined to provide new hope and a challenge for their young people who find themselves without work and who are often the victims of prejudice in their own society.

THINGS TO DO

1. Read the story of Jesus calling his first disciples in Mark's gospel, chapter 1 verses 14–20. Answer the following questions.
   (a) Where was Jesus teaching?
   (b) What was he saying?
   (c) Who were his first disciples?
   (d) What effect did Jesus have on people?
   Use this information to write a newspaper article set in Jesus' time called 'Who is this Jesus?'.

2. Jesus warned people about pride in an outward show of religion which may fool other people but which will not fool God. Read Matthew's Gospel, chaper 6 verses 1–18. Make a list of *four* things that please God according to this teaching and *four* things which do not please God. What is meant by the word 'hypocrite'? Discuss your answers in class.

3. Read the Lord's prayer in Matthew's Gospel, chapter 6 verses 9–13. Most Christians know this prayer by heart. Even very young children will know the words but may not fully understand them all. Write a simple version of the same prayer.

4. Find out about activities run by the churches in your area. Design a poster to put on a church notice board which advertises the activities run by the church.

5. Some people say that the church should keep out of political matters. Do you think that religion should stay out of politics? Discuss this question in pairs and then open the debate to the whole class.

6. In some churches the religious leader is called the **minister** or **pastor**. In the Catholic, Anglican and Orthodox traditions there are **priests**. Find out more about the work of a church minister or priest. Make up a set of interview questions to put to your local priest or minister. Write a TV programme called 'a day in the life of a priest/minister'.

27 The Church and churches

The word **church** has several meanings. It refers to the whole body of Christians and to the believers themselves. It also refers to a particular group of Christians, for example the **Methodists** are a church. 'Church' also refers to a building where Christians meet. There are many different kinds of church. By looking at different church buildings we can learn about the ways in which Christians express their faith. The first followers of Jesus met in a place called 'the upper room'. It was simply a room in someone's house. A church does not require anything special, just a group of faithful believers. Some Christians today meet in each others' homes to pray. Such groups are called **house churches**, the worship is informal and no priest is involved.

In a **Roman Catholic** church we find a formal setting (A). The **altar** is the focal point, it is a table representing the table of the Last Supper. Mass is central to Catholic worship. There is usually an organ and choir stalls. The **pulpit** is raised up in older churches and from here the sermon is given. At the back of the Catholic church there might be rooms where the priest hears confessions. There is also a **font** to hold the water for baptism. Many Catholic churches have a chapel dedicated to Mary the mother of Jesus which may be used for private prayer.

The **Anglican** church is quite like the Roman Catholic church. Again the focal point is the altar because Communion is important. There is often a pulpit on one side and a **lectern** for reading the scriptures on the other. Traditionally the font was near the door to symbolize entering the faith. There are modern Anglican and RC churches where the altar is at the centre and the seating is in a circle round it. The **Baptist** church has the pulpit in the most prominent position (B). The sermon and message of the Gospel given by the minister is important in Baptist worship and the Bible is read from here. Hidden from view, but also central, is the **baptistry** or pool. It is covered and empty except at baptisms when it is filled with water and becomes the focal point in the service.

A   *The altar is a focal point of a Roman Catholic Church*

27 The Church and churches

Many churches have a hall or building where they hold youth groups, coffee mornings, charity and other activities. Some churches were built to serve several purposes. The large Methodist halls found in most cities were built to be used for entertainment during the week. It was hoped this would bring more people to church on Sundays.

THINGS TO DO

1. Draw a map of your neighbourhood showing the different churches in the area. Find out when they were built.

2. Some Christian communities have had to adapt buildings such as old cinemas to set up a place for worship. Does a place of worship need to be a special or a beautiful place? Discuss this question in class and then write your answers.

3. Worshipping together has always been an important part of Christian practice. In what ways does the church bring people together? Design a plan for a church which helps to bring the community closer together, both in worship and in other activities. Write a few sentences to explain your design.

4. Some people feel it is a pity that there is division between the churches and that they should try to come together in unity. Do you agree? What difficulties would arise if different church groups tried to worship together? In what ways would it be a good thing to do? In what activities could the churches all get together if not in worship? Discuss these questions in class. Find out about the **Ecumenical Movement**.

5. Look at Photos A and B of the church interiors. Make a list of the similarities and differences between them. Say what these tell us about the beliefs and practices of the two churches.

6. Some city churches which were once filled with people every Sunday are no longer used. Imagine you lived near such a church. There are several groups wanting to buy the building.
   - The local bingo club needs bigger premises.
   - A developer wants to pull it down to build flats.
   - The Hindu community need a building for a place of worship.

   Work in groups, each being an interested party and one the local authority representative who decides on the matter. Debate what should happen to the church and take a vote at the end of the lesson.

B *Inside a Baptist church*

28 The Bible

Christians say Jesus Christ was 'the Word made Flesh'. They believe he acted out God's promise or word of love and forgiveness in his life. The Bible is also called the Word of God. Christians may read it at night before going to sleep or at the beginning of the day. Its words give comfort, guidance and inspiration. Many churches run Bible study groups and children learn the stories from the Bible at Sunday school.

The Bible has a special place in worship. In both the Anglican and Roman Catholic church there are readings from the Old and New Testaments in the services (A). When the Gospel is read at the service of Holy Communion the congregation stands as a sign of respect. In Orthodox churches the Bible is often beautifully bound and treated with great reverance and respect and is escorted by candles in a procession around the church (B).

A *The Bible is rested on a lectern in an Anglican church*

Christians call their scriptures the **Bible**. It contains a number of books. The largest section contains writings from the Jewish scriptures. The first Christians were Jewish and their scriptures were the Torah and Tenakh. They looked to these writings to try to understand everything that had happened concerning Jesus. These writings became a part of the Christian Bible, known as the **Old Testament**. The other section is called the **New Testament**. This contains writings by Christians. The best loved are the **Gospels**. These were written to inspire faith in Jesus Christ. They tell of his life and his teachings. Among the Christian writings are letters from St Paul and other church leaders who were writing to the first Christian communities. These contain words of guidance and comfort for members of the church. There are other writings too such as the book of Acts which preaches the message and story of the early church.

B *The Bible in a Greek Orthodox church*

28
The Bible

In other churches the service is often based on the Bible reading (C). The theme of the reading is echoed in the hymns and prayers. Members of the congregation may take their own Bibles to the service to follow the text. The preacher or visiting speaker uses all his expertise and energy to put across the teaching of the passage and to bring the words to life and make them meaningful. Christians believe that the words of the Bible have the power to bring people to faith in Jesus Christ. In some churches, worshippers who have been moved by the words of the scripture are invited to the front of the church to offer themselves to Christ. The minister lays his hands on their heads and others come forward to show their love and support in the same way.

THINGS TO DO

1. Look at a copy of the Bible. Note the difference between the New and Old Testaments. How are these two sections divided into smaller sections? Make a list of the different kinds of writings in the New Testament and give examples. Begin with the following headings.

Words of comfort and guidance for Christians	Stories about Jesus' life	Stories Jesus told

2. Study Photo B. How can we tell that this is no ordinary book? What does this tell you about the way these Christians regard their scriptures?

3. Some Christians believe that the Bible is literally, or word for word, true and everything happened exactly as it says. Others feel the message is sometimes given in symbols and stories which are not literally true. Read Luke's Gospel, chapter 9 verses 10–17. Some say that Jesus multiplied the bread and fishes. Others say it is a story about sharing. What does the text say? What miracle would take place if the food in the world were shared out? Discuss what you think the story is about.

4. The Bible has played an important part in influencing the life of this country and its people. Suggest ways in which the Bible has been an influence.

5. Draw the lectern. The eagle holding the globe represents the Gospel (i.e. the good news) and the world. Write a few sentences about the lectern and what it tells us about the importance of the Bible in Christian worship.

6. Most Christians would say that the Bible plays an important part in their lives. Invite a Christian to tell the class what the Bible means for them, when they read it and why.

C *A Free church minister preaching from the Bible*

29
Christian symbols

Signs and symbols can be powerful ways of conveying or expressing meaning. Some churches use many symbols in their worship. Others try to keep their worship simple. In a Society of Friends meeting house there is no altar, no cross, no picture, no image for worship (A). There is no written service and no priest, simply a set time and place to be silent and to share thoughts.

In contrast, some churches are elaborately decorated and their worship is rich in symbolism (B). In the Orthodox churches there are **icons** – pictures of Christ, **Mary** and the **saints** in glowing colours. Icons help carry the thoughts of the worshipper away from everyday matters to spiritual matters.

A *A Friends' Meeting House (Quaker)*

Roman Catholic churches often have images of **Mary** and other **saints**. Saints are men and women who dedicated their lives to the service of God. Catholics often light a candle beside the image and offer a prayer for someone they love. They feel they can approach Mary in their everyday prayers because she is the mother of Jesus. They feel she is very close to him and can communicate with him for them.

Some Christians believe that images and symbols distract the worshipper. They prefer to keep only those symbolic actions that Christ himself used such as the **breaking of bread**. Baptists use the symbol of **baptism** for new believers because Jesus taught his disciples to baptize in his name. When someone wants to commit their lives to Christ they are baptized by total immersion in water to symbolize dying and rising again with Christ. Some churches keep Jesus' command to wash each others' feet. This is a sign of humility and service to others.

The **cross** is the most universal Christian symbol. Christians believe that Jesus died on the cross for them, as a friend might give up his or her life to save someone they love. Some churches have a crucifix with the figure of Christ on it (C). This is often taken in a

29

Christian symbols

B *Inside an Orthodox church*

C *A crucifix carried in a procession*

procession on **Good Friday** when Christians remember the death of Jesus. Catholics and some Anglicans make the sign of the cross touching their forehead, chest, left shoulder and then right, saying, 'In the name of the **Father, Son** and **Holy Spirit**,' at the end of prayer or worship. These are the three aspects of God's nature and power. Christians sometimes wear the symbol of the cross on a chain to remember Jesus' love and self-sacrifice.

THINGS TO DO

1. Look at the differences between two churches (i.e. buildings). Working with a friend, make up a short interview with two Christians explaining the differences between their two places of worship.

2. Christians have tried to show Christ's divine and human nature in pictures and images. Find illustrations of the ways people have pictured Christ. Discuss the different images.

3. Read John's Gospel, chapter 13 verses 3–17. What does this symbolic action tell us about: (a) Jesus, (b) Peter, and (c) the way Christians are meant to behave towards others?

4. In some churches the priest wears special clothes. Invite your local vicar to explain about the symbolism of the robes and other symbols in the Anglican church. Make a class display of Christian symbols.

5. Some people feel that images, icons and pictures can be a problem because they come between the worshipper and God. Do images help or hinder worship? Debate this question in class.

6. Draw the different ways in which the symbol of the cross appears and write a few sentences about its meaning.

30 The Christian year

Christmas and **Easter** are the two great landmarks of the Christian year. The Christian calendar follows the life of Christ. It begins with **Advent**, a time of preparation before the coming of Christ at Christmas. The birth of Jesus is celebrated on Christmas Day. It is a family festival and Christians remember the holy family of Mary, Joseph and Jesus. The mystery of God made Man is expressed in the story of the Christ child, weak and helpless yet an object of adoration and love.

The Christmas season ends with the feast of **Epiphany** on 6 January. In the Catholic and Anglican churches this marks the story of the **magi** or wise men visiting Jesus with gifts of gold, frankincense and myrrh. In the **Eastern** and **Orthodox** tradition Epiphany celebrates three events in the story of Jesus: the adoration of the magi, the baptism of Jesus and his first miracle. Epiphany means 'manifestation' or making known. On these three occasions it was made known who Jesus really was. Special services are held in Orthodox churches at Epiphany and families celebrate with presents and festive foods.

The most important festival in the church year is Easter. It commemorates the death and **resurrection** of Jesus. There are six weeks of preparation called **Lent**. This used to be a time of fasting and repentance. Today, Christians still say sorry to God for all they have done wrong but few people fast. **Good Friday** is a day of mourning and Christians meditate on Christ's death. Between Good Friday and Easter Day, many Christians keep a vigil in their church. At dawn on the Sunday, candles are lit to symbolize Jesus overcoming death and rising to life.

Ascension Day is another important landmark in the Christian year. It commemorates the occasion when Christ left his disciples for the last time to return to God. He commanded his followers to continue his work on earth. He also promised the gift of the Holy Spirit which would be his presence and power on earth. **Whitsun** commemorates the disciples receiving the Holy Spirit at **Pentecost**

A *Festival in the Orthodox tradition*

30 The Christian year

(50 days after the Jewish Passover). The story tells of the Spirit coming like a rush of wind and settling like flames on the disciples. This marked the birth of the church. The sign of the Holy Spirit was accompanied with the **gift of tongues**. This was a special way of communicating; the disciples spoke in languages they had never learnt. **Pentecostal** churches still practise speaking in tongues. The worshippers allow themselves to be 'moved by the spirit' and express themselves with shouts of praise (B). Others give voice to words and sounds which do not make sense in the normal way of speaking. In the past Whitsun was a popular time for baptizing new believers. They wore white, and the name 'White Sunday' or 'Whitsun' arose.

The Christian year follows the life of Christ and the birth of the church, so believers learn about the faith, its history and its teachings through the festivals and seasons of the church.

THINGS TO DO

1. Look up the stories of Epiphany: Matthew's Gospel chapter 2 verses 1–23, chapter 3 verses 13–17 and John's Gospel chapter 2 verses 1–11. What do these tell us about what Christians believe? Design a poster advertising the feast of Epiphany at an Orthodox church. Illustrate the stories and their meaning.

2. Make a comparison between the celebration of Krishna's birthday in Hinduism and the festival of Christmas. What are the similarities between the two stories and the two festivals?

3. Design a chart of the Christian year with an illustration or symbol marking each season and festival.

4. In a sense every Sunday is a mini-Easter. Jesus rose from the dead on a Sunday. The Jewish Sabbath falls on Saturday. Jesus' followers were Jewish. They were so convinced about the Resurrection of Jesus that they changed the Sabbath to mark the event. What does this tell you about the Easter experience? How can Sunday become a mini-Easter for Christians?

5. Easter is the most important festival in the Christian year. Deep human questions about life and death, suffering and sin are raised in the Easter story. Find out what Christians believe in answer to the questions below (not all Christians will agree on these matters).
   - Is there life after death?
   - How do we know?
   - How should we live our lives?
   - If there is a God does he understand what it is like to suffer or die?

6. Imagine you belong to a Christian family. What would be your favourite times in the Church year? Explain, giving the meaning and the symbolism of the different festivals.

B *A Pentecostal church service*

31
A plan for all

A *Reading from the Qur'an*

B *Children in classes at the mosque*

Muslims are followers of the faith of Islam. Islam means submission; it can also mean peace. A Muslim is someone who submits themselves to the will of **Allah**. Allah is the Islamic word for God. According to Islam, everyone has a choice in life. People can follow their own selfish way or they can follow the way of Allah. Muslims believe that Allah created the world and all living beings. They believe Allah loves his creation and wants men and women to choose the path that is best for them.

In our society we are often encouraged to put ourselves first. We are told to 'be independent' or 'think for yourself'. The emphasis is on the individual. In Islam, as in other religions, men and women are called to put God first and submit to his will and his plan. Islam requires individuals to see themselves as a part of a community and recognize that Allah's plan takes into account the needs of the community as well as those of the individual. This plan is found in the teachings of the **Qur'an**.

The word Qur'an means 'recitation'. Muslims believe it contains Allah's final and most perfect revelation. Its teachings offer guidance for every aspect of life from how to pray to what food to eat, from how to run a business to the way to govern. In this way religion is not separate from everyday living. The laws and teachings of the Qur'an are guidelines not only for individuals but for the whole of society. Muslims believe that it is the most complete revelation of Allah's will.

Most Muslims have a copy of the Qur'an. They treat it with the greatest reverence. A Muslim will never put the Qur'an on the floor. The Qur'an is always given a place higher than other books in a room and if it is not being read it is wrapped in a cloth. When a Muslim goes to read the Qur'an he or she will first wash and cover their head to show reverence for the word of Allah (A). The text is in Arabic (C). Muslims learn the language to read and recite from their scriptures. They believe that the full

31
A plan for all

and teaching of **Muhammad (Pbuh)**. It is not considered as important or sacred as the holy Qur'an but its wealth of teaching plays an important part in Muslim life and education.

When Muslims use the name of Muhammad they follow it with **Pbuh**, which means 'Peace be upon him'. This is why his name is printed like this the first time it is used in each of these units.

THINGS TO DO

1 Look at Photo A. How can you tell that this is not an ordinary book that is being read? Make a list of all the clues. Discuss the points you have in class.

2 Sometimes the Qur'an is read from a stand. Make a model Qur'an stand. You need two identical cardboard supports with a slit cut half way through each so that they slot together. Decorate it with patterns cut out or coloured in.

3 Imagine you are a Muslim and you bring your Qur'an in to school. How would you show and explain to your friends the way you treat your Qur'an as something holy? What difficulties would arise for you in keeping the Qur'an in school? Write what you would do and say.

4 Our own selfish plans in life may not take into account the needs of others. Muslims believe that Allah's plan takes into account the fact that everything we do affects others in some way. List 10 things you do each day. With a friend decide which of these things could affect or influence other people.

5 Where do you get your guidelines for life? What influences the way you think and act? Draw yourself, in the middle of a large page. Use arrows, symbols and pictures to show the people and things which influence and guide your life.

6 Muslims learn to read and write Arabic from an early age (B). Try to write out the Arabic alphabet. In a few sentences explain why Muslim children have to learn Arabic.

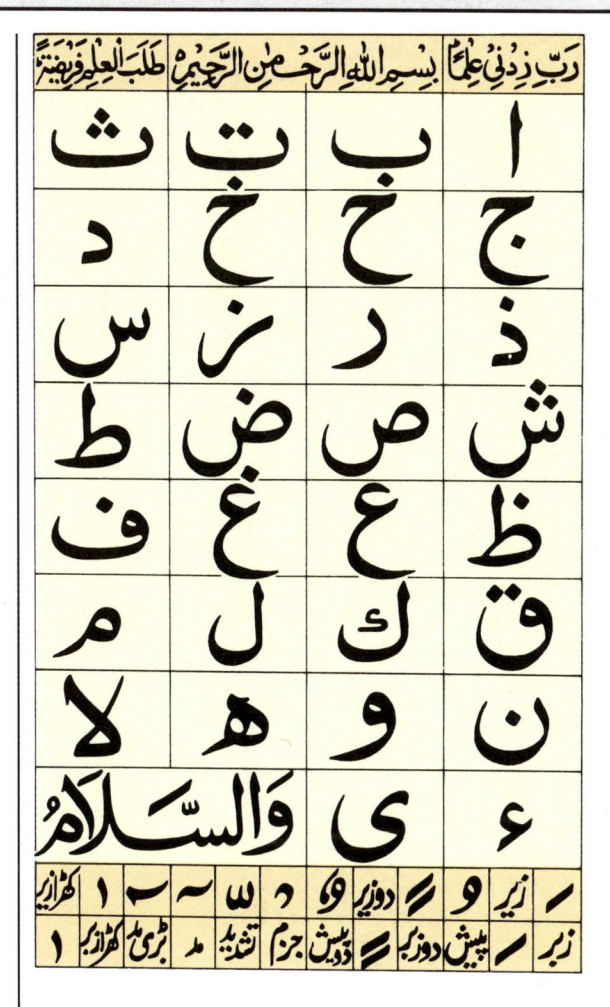

C *Some of the symbols from the Arabic alphabet*

meaning of the Qur'an can only be understood in its original Arabic. Some Muslims learn the entire text by heart and receive the name **hafiz**. The text is divided into **surahs** or chapters and the surahs are in verses. There is a flow and rhythm in the Arabic giving the Qur'an a special power and beauty. The words are intended to draw the reader or listener to worship Allah as Creator and Lord of the universe.

Muslims live their lives according to the teachings of the Qur'an. They also find guidance in another text called the **Hadith**. This is a collection of stories and sayings from the life

32
The Holy Qur'an

The Qur'an says that when Allah first created men and women he showed them the way to live. In time, however, the people fell into evil ways and ignored their creator. Allah sent his prophets Nuh, Ibrahim, Moses and others including Jesus to bring the people back to the right path. The people took no notice and continued in their selfish way of life. Eventually Allah gave his message to **Muhammad (Pbuh)**. The account of Muhammad receiving the words of the Qur'an is a story of Allah's love because according to Muslims the words of the Qur'an are Allah's most precious gift to the world.

Muhammad was born in 570 CE in **Makkah** in Arabia (A). By the age of six he was an orphan and was brought up by his uncle Abu Talib. He belonged to the Quraish tribe. He took up work as a trader for a successful business woman called Khadijah. She proposed to him and they married. On his travels Muhammad met and talked with Jews and Christians whose scriptures taught that there was only one God. Muhammad had long since become depressed by the corrupt religious practices of the people of Makkah. Their worship seemed empty and meaningless. The sacred building, the **Ka'ba** in Makkah had once been dedicated to the One True God. It had since become a place for selling idols and souvenirs from which Muhammad's own tribe made a huge profit.

Muhammad began to spend time on his own in a mountain cave outside Makkah. He devoted himself to prayer and fasting. During this time Muhammad was called by Allah to be a prophet. While he was alone the angel Gabriel visited him. He came very close and commanded Muhammad, 'recite.' Muhammad protested that he could neither read nor write. Again the angel told him, 'Recite,' and as he did so he squeezed him. Muhammad protested again that he could not. A third time the angel commanded him to recite and squeezed him. This time Muhammad knew that the words were on his lips ready to be spoken.

> Recite,
> In the name of thy Lord who created –
> Created man from a clot of blood.
> Recite,
> For thy Lord is bountiful,
> Who taught by the pen,
> Taught man what he knew not.

A   A map showing the positions of Madinah and Makkah

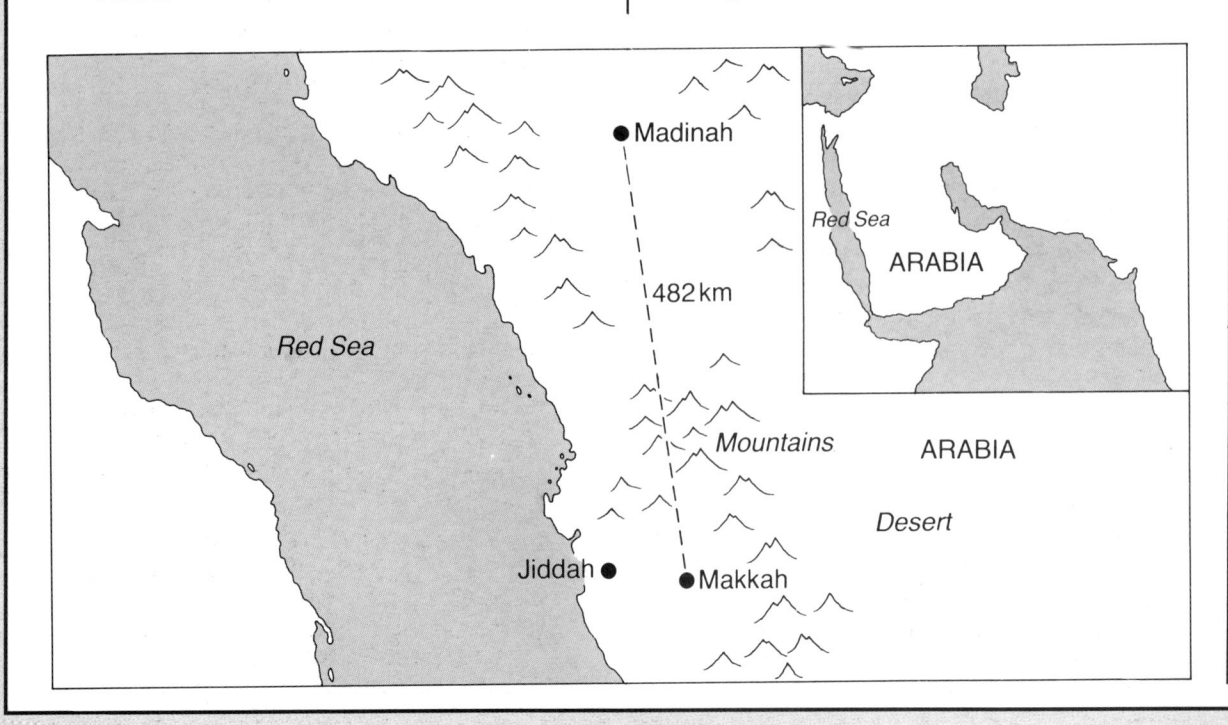

32
The Holy Qur'an

B *The Qur'an is kept covered when not being read*

The angel Gabriel returned many times and Muhammad received all the words of the Holy Qur'an. Muhammad told Khadijah his wife about his visits from the angel. She believed him to be the prophet of Allah and became the first Muslim woman. Abu Bakr, Muhammad's friend, also believed him. Muhammad began to preach to the people of Makkah. He told them that Allah was the One True God and that they should worship only Allah and turn from their evil ways.

THINGS TO DO

1. Some things are very precious to us because they are very old or because someone special gave them. Describe your most precious possession. Explain how you treat it differently from other things you have. Compare your notes with a friend.

C *A page from the Qur'an*

2. The story of Muhammad tells us why the Qur'an is so precious for Muslims (B). Give a brief account of the story and explain what it tells us about the Qur'an.

3. Some copies of the Qur'an are illuminated with elaborate designs such as abstract patterns or plants and flowers (C). No human figures or creatures are used. This is to avoid making idols. Allah is too great to picture. Copy the verse of the Qur'an from the text and illuminate it. Explain the design.

4. What is a prophet? The different religions have different ideas. Who were prophets in the past? Are there any prophets now? What would you look for in a prophet? What would you expect them to do? Do you think people would listen to a prophet today? Discuss this in class.

5. Invite a Muslim to visit your class to show you the Qur'an and to talk about why it is important to them. If you are allowed to handle the Qur'an remember to wash your hands first. Ask them to read some of the verses in Arabic for you.

6. Muhammad's birthday is marked in some countries by a public holiday. Muhammad is not worshipped in any way but he is very important. In what ways is he important? Find out more about Muhammad and write a paragraph on his importance for Muslims.

33
Five Pillars

Worship can be private or public. It can involve words or actions or be expressed in other ways. In Islam there are five ways in which a Muslim is expected to serve and worship God. These are called the **Five Pillars**.

Shahadah is the first of these pillars. Shahadah is saying the most important beliefs of the faith: 'I bear witness that there is no God but Allah and I bear witness that Muhammad (Pbuh) is the messenger of Allah.' This statement makes it clear that Muslims believe there is only one God. They do not believe God has a son. Muhammad is a man, not a divine person. He was the last of God's prophets and his life is an example to follow but he is not to be worshipped. Only Allah is to be worshipped.

The second pillar is **salah**. Salah is prayer. Muslims should pray five times a day at set times (A). In this way Allah is remembered throughout the day every day.

B *Ramadan in a Muslim country*

The third of the pillars is **saum** or fasting. Muslims are expected to fast during the month of **Ramadan**. As Muslims use a lunar calendar Ramadan falls at a different time each year. Saum means going without food or water during the hours of daylight for a month each year (B). The whole person observes the fast: mind and body. Eyes, ears, heart, hands must all refrain from evil. Spiritual matters are put first and time is spent at the mosque in prayer and reading the Qur'an.

Zakah is the fourth pillar of Islam. Zakah is charity (C). Every Muslim is expected to serve Allah in this way because it is a part of Allah's plan to see that all members of the community are cared for. Muslims believe that everything in the world is a gift from Allah. It is Allah's will that those who have wealth should share with those who have nothing. In this way they are following the example of Allah's generosity.

A *Muslims at prayer*

33
Five Pillars

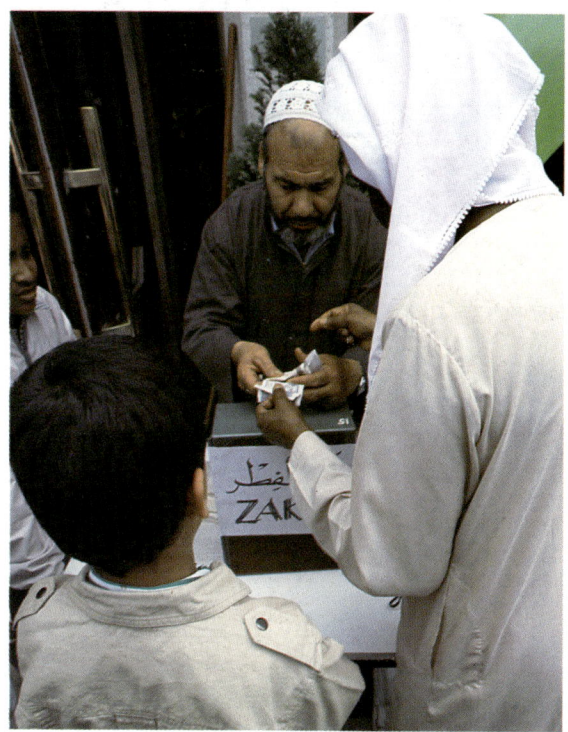

C A zakat collecting box

Charity stops people from being too greedy and selfish and discourages feelings of envy and pride. Roughly speaking, everyone is expected to give $2\frac{1}{2}$ per cent of their savings.

The last pillar is **Hajj**. This is the pilgrimage to the holy city of Makkah at least once in a life time, if money and health allow. Hajj is an act of worship, to renew faith through devoting time, money and energy to Allah. It is an act of sacrifice and a time to give up worldly matters completely and to think about Allah.

THINGS TO DO

1. Make a poster of the Five Pillars using the idea of pillars to hold up faith, and explaining the words shahadah, salah, saum, zakah and Hajj.

2. Islam means submission. Imagine you are a Muslim and you have been asked to explain Islam. Write a talk to say how the Five Pillars help you lead a life of submission to Allah.

3. Keeping the Five Pillars can be hard. Sometimes difficulty and struggle can help us to learn something about life or ourselves. Describe an occasion when you have learnt something through hardship or difficulties.

4. Zakah is distributed to the poor, both Muslim and non-Muslim. Work out how much you would have to give if you saved half of your pocket money each week for a year. How would you feel about giving $2\frac{1}{2}$ per cent away? It is said that zakah purifies the giver. In what way could this be true? Discuss this in class.

5. In countries where the majority of people are Muslim, life is organized to take account of the Five Pillars (B). What difficulties do you think Muslims meet in Britain keeping the Five Pillars of Islam? Write a magazine article called 'A Muslim in Britain'.

6. Revise or find out what you can about Ramadan and Hajj. Make up a set of questions on these topics to swap with a friend.

34 Salah

Salah is usually translated as prayer. Salah is not personal prayer but organized worship. It is a set of words and actions which focus the mind and body on Allah. The mind is easily distracted and the body is full of desires and needs. Prayer is not easy. If a person wants to concentrate on God they must put all other thoughts and desires to one side. The routine of salah helps the worshipper to do this.

Muslims are called to prayer five times a day (A). These times are early morning, noon, mid-afternoon, sunset and night. The exact times are given at the mosque. A **muezzin** recites the **adhan** or 'call to prayer' from the **minaret**. In preparation for prayer Muslims must wash. This is called **wudu** (B). This is not only to cleanse the body but also the mind. As they wash their face, mouth, nose, ears, hands and feet Muslims think about the things they should not have said or done and purify their hearts and minds.

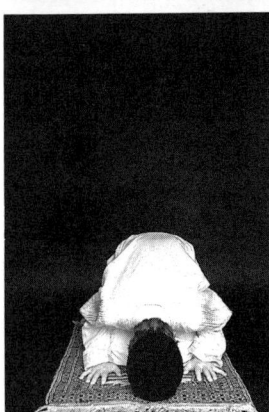

A *Prayer positions*

B *Muslims washing before prayer*

Muslims remove their shoes for prayer. There are carpets or mats at the mosque (C). Most muslims also have their own prayer carpet so they can pray no matter where they are. At the mosque it is usual for Muslims to cover their heads. Women must dress modestly, covering their arms, legs and hair. Often there is a separate gallery for women to

34
Salah

pray. Muslims face in the direction of Makkah for salah.

Once the worshipper is ready, he or she expresses an intention to follow through one, two or more units of prayer. Each unit is called a **rak'ah**. It consists of words and movements. A rak'ah begins with the recitation of 'God is Great' in Arabic and verses from the Qur'an are recited. Muslims can perform salah alone but most Muslim men try to pray at the mosque when they can. At the Mosque the prayers are usually said in unison. Men stand shoulder to shoulder facing Makkah. It is a sign of equality as no one is meant to stick their chests out in pride or try to separate themselves from their fellow worshippers. The sound of voices praying together is soft and low and the hushed movements of the prayer positions express the total submission of the worshippers to Allah. There is a special atmosphere of peace and unity at the mosque when Muslims pray. After completing salah Muslims turn their heads to the right and left saying to their neighbour, 'Peace be upon you and the mercy of Allah.' They may go on to say their own private prayers.

C *A Muslim prayer carpet*

THINGS TO DO

1. Imagine you are a Muslim. You have been asked to write about salah for the school magazine so that other pupils understand Muslim prayer. Use words and pictures in your article.

2. The following things are important in Islam. How are they expressed in salah?
   - submission
   - humility
   - concentration
   - purity
   - unity
   - sincerity
   - brotherhood
   - peace

   Work out your answers in pairs using the text and photos to help you.

3. Salah is not always easy to perform at the given times. Can you think when and why it might be difficult? How could schools and places of work make it easier for Muslims to perform salah? Discuss these questions in class.

4. According to tradition, Muhammad (Pbuh) was taken on a spiritual journey from Makkah to Jerusalem. He ascended to paradise and met with Ibrahim (Abraham) and the prophets. Here Muhammad was given the commandment for prayer. At first it was to be 500 times a day. But this would be too hard for people, so Allah suggested 50. Muhammad pointed out how weak human beings were, so it came to be five times a day. Muslims call this occasion the **Night of Power**. Mosques and minarets are lit up, prayers are held and stories about Muhammad are remembered. Design a card or leaflet advertising the Night of Power at the mosque.

5. Draw a design for a prayer carpet. It must not have any people or creatures in the pattern. Some rugs have a picture of the Ka'ba or the Dome of the Rock pictured in the design.

6. Worship can take many different forms. List the different expressions of worship you have learnt about. Which religions use which expressions? Make a chart to show this.

35 The mosque

A *A mosque in Lahore, Pakistan*

Muslims are meant to pray together whenever they can. **Mosque** means a place of prostration or prayer. Muslims try to attend the mosque daily but especially for salah midday on Fridays for **Jum'ah** prayers (A). Friday is not a holy day but Friday prayers are important because the **imam** gives a sermon on this occasion. In the Hadith Muhammad (Pbuh) says, 'If a person takes a bath on Friday, washes himself thoroughly, oils his hair . . . sets forth for the mosque, does not intrude between two persons, offers the prescribed prayer and listens to the imam, his sins committed since the previous Friday are forgiven.'

Mosques vary from place to place. There is always a large room for prayer and there are no seats, just carpets. One wall of the mosque, called the **qiblah**, is marked with a niche to indicate the direction of Makkah. This niche is called the **mihrab**. At the entrance there is a place for worshippers to leave their shoes and there is running water for washing.

Many mosques are recognizable from the outside as the minaret stands out. From here the muezzin calls people to prayer. Sometimes there is a dome. This helps to circulate the air in the prayer hall. Some say it represents the universe. There may be a crescent moon on the top but it has no special religious meaning except as a symbol of Islam. In this country mosques are often converted houses or halls (B and C).

At the mosque an **imam** leads the worshippers for salat. The imam has no special status. He may know the teachings of the Qur'an better than most and he might therefore be called upon to advise members of the Muslim community when they have questions or problems. The imam may also run classes at the mosque. Children attend the mosque during the week to learn Arabic and read the Qur'an. Most children have their own copy of the Qur'an which they take with them, wrapped in a cloth cover. Children cover their heads at the

35
The mosque

mosque, boys wear a small cap and the girls wear a scarf over their head and shoulders. The older children often help the imam in teaching the younger ones. In Britain the mosque is often where family celebrations are held. At festive times the mosque is an ideal place for people to get together. Some mosques are cultural or community centres for the Muslim population (C). However, the mosque is primarily a place for prayer and for studying the Qur'an.

THINGS TO DO

1. Design a small information leaflet on 'The mosque' using pictures, diagrams and writing to explain the design and function of the building.

2. Look at the photos in this unit. Make a note of the differences between the mosques. Can you think of reasons for these?

3. The Muslim community in Britain is drawn together in a special way at the mosque. Why is this? Imagine you are a Muslim. You enjoy going to the mosque to learn but also to meet with your friends and talk. Describe what the mosque means for you as a Muslim living in Britain.

4. Most young Muslims in Britain were born and educated here and are British citizens. Their grandparents or their parents may have originally come from Pakistan, Bangladesh or India. The mosque in Britain is often different from the mosques in these countries. Imagine you are a young Muslim. Write a letter to a penfriend in Pakistan. Describe your local mosque and neighbourhood. Use the photos to help you.

5. If you were to take a class trip to a mosque, how would you have to prepare for your visit? Design a set of guidelines for teachers taking children to visit a mosque. Invite a Muslim to speak to the class about the place and importance of the mosque in Islam or, if you can, arrange a visit to a mosque. Prepare a set of questions you would want to ask.

6. Imagine you are a Muslim going to Jum'ah prayers. Describe how you prepare and what you do at the mosque.

B *A mosque in Britain*

C *The mosque as a community centre*

36
The Muslim world

A *A Geometric Muslim design*

Islam stresses the importance of the equality of all people no matter whether they are black or white, rich or poor and regardless of where they are from. Perhaps it is partly for this reason that the faith was able to spread so rapidly. When Muhammad (Pbuh) began preaching in Makkah some believed him, others turned against him because he was ruining their trade in idols. Muhammad migrated to the city of **Madinah** until a better time. He was welcomed and invited to be their leader and establish peace in a city torn apart by quarrels. Muhammad united the people through faith in one God. He was accepted as a prophet and a leader and so began the first Muslim community.

Muhammad's thoughts returned to Makkah. He set about trying to enter the city. He made persistent efforts to persuade the Makkans to let him return. After resisting attacks from their armies he was eventually allowed to talk with the leaders of Makkah. It was agreed that Muhammad should return to establish peace and unity. The first thing Muhammad did was to dedicate the **Ka'ba** again to Allah (C). Once he had the loyalty of Makkah the way was open to reach the rest of Arabia.

Muhammad died in 632 CE. His faithful follower Abu Bakr continued his work and became the first **caliph** or successor. Within a century of Muhammad's death Islam had reached Spain in the West and Afghanistan in the East. As Islam spread its influence could be seen in art and architecture, in science and mathematics. Representing figures of people is discouraged in Islam, so art developed in the form of fine calligraphy and geometric pattern (A). From this design work grew expertise in geometry and mathematics. As Islam spread it was important to work out the direction of Makkah from different parts of the globe. This led to a greater understanding of geography and the movements of the stars and planets which enabled Muslims to pinpoint the direction of Makkah from anywhere in the Muslim world (B). The Arabic numeral system was far less clumsy than the Roman one and soon replaced it. In places Islam brought peace, unity and stability where there had previously been unrest, so art and science were able to flourish.

B *An astrolabe, used to find the direction of Makkah, shows the early advancement in science and understanding of the globe in the Muslim world*

36
The Muslim world

C *The Ka'ba at Makkah*

THINGS TO DO

1. Draw and colour an example of Islamic geometric design such as is found in the decoration of mosques. Write a sentence or two about it.

2. The unity of Muslims is expressed in many ways in their life and worship. Make a list of all the ways in which the 'oneness', unity and equality of all Muslims finds expression.

3. Muslims do not believe that God took human form. They do not accept that God has a son. Jesus is seen as a prophet. Islam is strictly monotheistic. This means belief in one God only and no other divine being. Which religions are monotheistic? Discuss this in the class.

4. The Ka'ba is an important symbol for Muslims (C). Why is this? How do Muslims show its importance? Make a postcard of the Ka'ba. Write a message on the back as a Muslim parent writing from Makkah to your children about having seen the Ka'ba.

5. Islam has had an enormous influence on the world. Find out more about art, architecture, mathematics and science in the Muslim world. Prepare a class project on one of these topics.

6. The majority of Muslims are Sunni Muslims and there are a minority called Shi'i. The Shi'ites rejected the leadership of the first caliphs and made a descendent of Muhammad their leader. Despite this division there is no difference in their basic beliefs and worship. Religion can unite or divide. List the way in which religions unite people. Discuss ways in which religions can also divide people.

37
In the home

The majority of young Muslims in this country were born here. Their families may have originally come from Pakistan, India or Bangladesh. The Muslim home is influenced by the teachings of the Qur'an, by the society around them and by the family background. Muslims begin the day by washing and preparing for dawn prayers. Men go to pray at the local mosque. Women pray at home. As in many families the woman is usually responsible for looking after the home. Muslim women may also have a career or go to work (A). They are expected to dress modestly, keeping their arms and legs covered in the presence of men outside the family. Many Muslim women prefer a job where they will be working with women only. Muhammad said paradise was to be found at the feet of the mother. The Qur'an gives women the right to inherit, to own land and the same right to education as men. Women received status and respect in Islam at a time when they had few rights in society at large.

Diet varies from one Muslim home to another. Pork is forbidden in the Qur'an, and alcohol is too. Muslims are required to eat only **halal** meat which has been slaughtered so that the blood is drained and God's name has been said as the animal is killed (C). There are now many halal butchers in Britain where Muslims can buy meat. In the home, children learn the teachings of the Qur'an and listen to stories about Muhammad. They watch and follow their parents' example in prayer and learn to recite the words of the Qur'an. Grandparents may live with the family and help to bring up the children in the faith. Muslims believe that it is a duty to care for and respect their elderly.

Muslim families are brought together in a special way during the month of Ramadan when they learn to help each other through the difficulties of fasting. Festivals are important family occasions too. The most important is **Eid ul Fitr**, the day of thanksgiving and celebration at the end of Ramadan.

Another important occasion is **Eid ul Adha**, the festival of sacrifice (B). The night before this is spent in prayer and reading the Qur'an. In the morning Muslims attend the mosque.

A *A girl dressed in shalwar and kameez*

37
In the home

Every family buys an animal for sacrifice at Eid ul Adha. The animal is slaughtered and the meat is shared with the poor so that they too may celebrate. It is a day of thanksgiving. It marks the occasion when Ibrahim proved his faith in God by his willingness to sacrifice his own son. Eid ul Adha falls during the Hajj and is an important part of the pilgrimage. Muslims remember that faith requires sacrifice and obedience.

THINGS TO DO

1. It is in the home that children become familiar with the beliefs and practices of the faith. Imagine you are a British Muslim. Write a letter to a penfriend describing your daily routine, your home and your family.

2. There are many people who would be disappointed if there were a law to prevent people from drinking alcohol here. There are many who would be pleased, relieved or even grateful. Discuss who these might be and what reasons they would give.

3. Find out more about life in a Muslim home and the teachings of the Qur'an on (a) food, (b) dress, and (c) parents and children. Design an illustrated pamphlet on these.

4. Islam teaches that the young are to respect their elders and families are to look after the elderly. Most elderly people like to look after themselves and not be a burden on anyone. They can play an important part in family life. Do you think children respect their elders? What is meant by 'respect'? What part can grandparents play in bringing up children in the faith of the family? Discuss these points in class.

5. The sacrifice at Eid ul Adha reminds Muslims that faith means willing to sacrifice everything for God. What things in life would be most hard to give up: money? independence? time? luxuries? Make a list of things which you would find difficult to give up.

6. Muslim parents take their children's education very seriously and the mosque offers classes and activities for the young so that they learn not to be ashamed to be Muslim. Design a poster encouraging young people to be proud of their family faith.

B *Celebration of Eid*

C *A Muslim family at the Halal butcher's*

38

Guru Nanak

Many people keep or wear a memento from someone they admire or love. It may be a locket or a piece of clothing. Wearing the memento is important. It gives the wearer a feeling of closeness to the person they love and acts as a constant reminder of them. Wearing something in this way is a symbol of love or faithfulness. Sikhs have been given special things to wear as a sign of faithfulness. They are called the **five Ks**: **kesh, kanga, kachs, kirpan** and **kara**. These symbols are an outward sign of an inward love and commitment to God.

Sikh means 'learner'. A Sikh might be described as a disciple or pupil who is seeking to know God. Sikhs do this by following the path laid down by the **Ten Gurus**. The Ten Gurus were the founders of Sikhism. The first Guru was Guru Nanak (A).

Guru Nanak was born in 1469 in the Indian village of Talwandi. It is now in Pakistan. Guru Nanak's father was a Hindu. He worked as an accountant to the village landlord who was a Muslim. From an early age Guru Nanak showed unusual devotion to God. He spent many hours in meditation, prayer and singing devotional hymns. He grew up with two friends Bala, who was a Hindu, and Mardana, a Muslim. Guru Nanak was an unselfish child. He was always putting the needs of others before his own. Once, his father sent him into the city to find a bargain and make a good exchange. He gave his son 20 rupees. On the way Guru Nanak met 20 starving holy men. He gave them the money to buy food. When Guru Nanak returned his father was angry but Guru Nanak said he had made a 'good' exchange.

The best loved story of Guru Nanak's life is about the time he mysteriously vanished. He had been in the river bathing before dawn prayers. Three days passed and Guru Nanak then reappeared. He said he had stood in the presence of God and had been sent to call people to true worship and brotherhood. So Guru Nanak devoted the rest of his life to God. He travelled throughout India, teaching and singing God's praises, accompanied by his

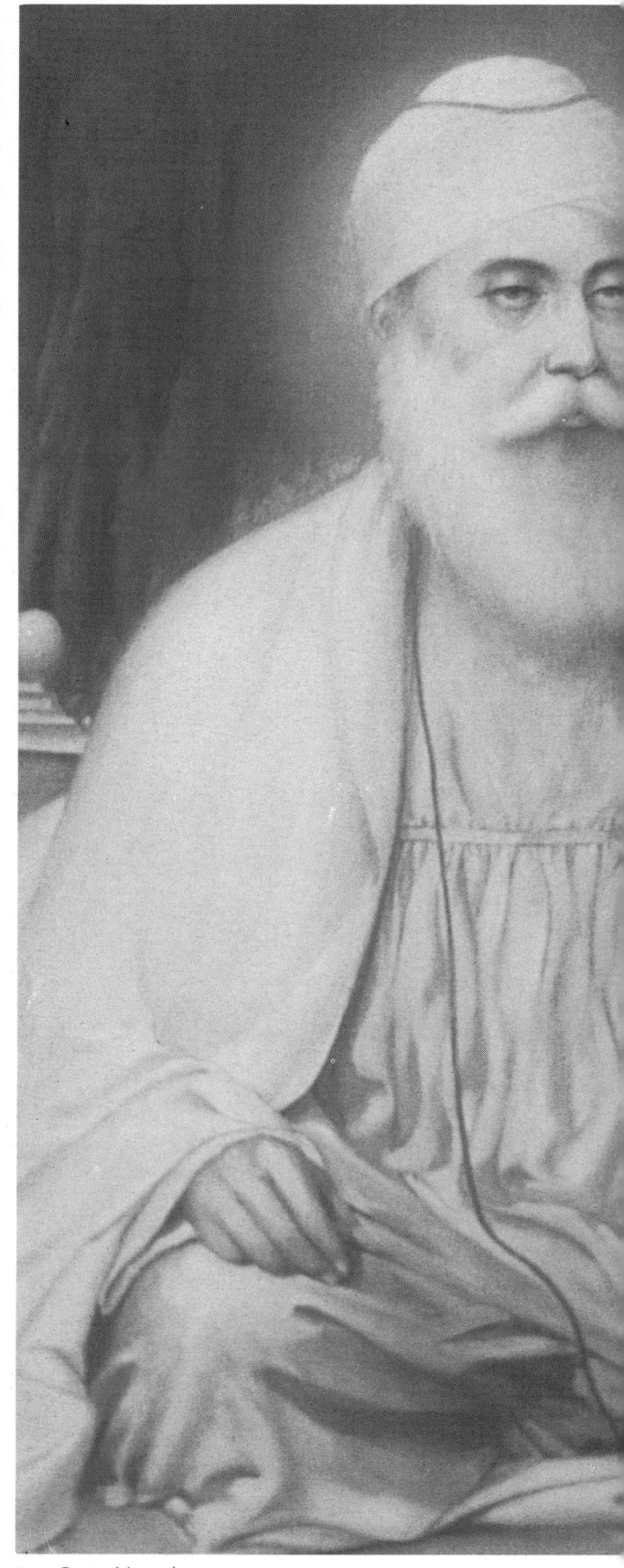

A *Guru Nanak*

38
Guru Nanak

friend and musician Mardana. Guru Nanak set up a community of followers at Kartarpur who treasured his teachings and followed his example of devotion to God and service to others.

Before his death, Guru Nanak entrusted a successor to continue his work and his teaching. In all there were to be nine successors. Finally, the tenth Guru said there would be no further human guru. Instead the teachings of the gurus would become like a living guru among them. These teachings are in the Sikh holy book, the **Guru Granth Sahib**.

B *A Sikh in Britain*

THINGS TO DO

1 Revise the five Ks. Make a list of *six* things people wear which have special meaning for them. Write a sentence or two about each one, illustrating them if you wish.

2 Kesh, uncut hair, is a sign of the Sikh's commitment to God. Sikhs wear turbans to keep it in place. Look at Photo B of the man wearing his turban at work. What does this picture tell you about the man's attitude and faith?

3 The turban makes Sikh men identifiable. Are people of other faiths recognizable by what they wear? What difficulties could this cause? Can we make sure that people are not made to feel uncomfortable about their religions and culture? Discuss this in class.

4 Guru Nanak is often called **Guruji**; 'ji' is a term of respect. Sometimes he is known affectionately as **Baba Nanak**. Imagine you are writing a book for Sikh children. Choose one episode from Guru Nanak's life and tell it in words and pictures. Say what it tells us about Guru Nanak.

5 Guru Nanak rose before dawn to pray. What is the world like before dawn? Describe it in a poem or prose. Why would this be a good time for quiet thought, prayer or meditation?

6 When Guru Nanak returned after his disappearance he said, 'There is no Hindu and there is no Muslim; whose religion shall I follow? I shall follow God's religion.' What do you think he meant by this? How did he demonstrate this in his life? Discuss these questions in class.

39
A living Guru

The **Guru Granth Sahib** is the Sikh holy book (A). The words of the Guru Granth Sahib are believed to be from God, received by the gurus. They are hymns and teachings in verse form. The Guru Granth Sahib represents the living word of the gurus and is given the honour due to a living guru. Few Sikhs own a copy of the scriptures as the Guru Granth Sahib requires a room of its own. Most Sikhs go to the **gurdwara**, their place of worship, to hear their scriptures.

At the gurdwara, the Guru Granth Sahib is enthroned. It is read from a platform or dais called a **takht**. In this way the scriptures are given a position of authority and respect. The takht is cushioned for the reader. On the takht is a small stool called the **manji sahib**. This too is covered and cushioned to hold the holy book in position. There is often a canopy over the scriptures. When prepared for reading the Guru Granth Sahib is laid on the cushions and unwrapped from its silken coverings. The pages are opened carefully and a **chauri** or fan is waved reverently over the text. This was once a sign of homage shown to royalty and holy men. The chauri is made from yak hair, feathers or nylon. When the scriptures are not being read, they are wrapped again and carried head high to a bed of cushions (B). Prayers are said as the holy book is laid to rest.

The Guru Granth Sahib plays an essential part in the life of every Sikh. The hymns are cherished and recited daily. They offer hope and comfort in times of trouble and words of courage and guidance for everyday life. The teachings of the gurus describe the nature of God and proclaim his love for those who devote

A *The Guru Granth Sahib*

B *Carrying the Guru Granth Sahib*

39
A living Guru

C The Guru Granth Sahib, takht and canopy

themselves to his service. Sikhs worship one God. They call him **Sat Guru** or the True Guru. Sometimes he is called **Sat Nam**, the sacred Name of God. Many Sikhs have a small book of the best loved hymns from the scriptures. Most Sikhs know many by heart and use them in prayer.

The Guru Granth Sahib is the focal point at the gurdwara in all public worship, at festivals and family celebrations. Its texts are recited in Punjabi from the ancient Gurmukhi script. Sikhs believe a translation could not do justice to the poetry and meaning of the words.

THINGS TO DO

1 Look at Photo A of the Sikh holy scriptures. Draw a diagram of the Guru Granth Sahib on the takht. Show the canopy and the granthi holding the chauri. Label your picture and learn the new vocabulary.

2 **Guru** means teacher or someone who leads you from 'darkness' into 'light'. Why do you think the Sikh holy book is referred to as the Guru? Describe the ways in which the Guru Granth Sahib is treated as a living guru. Use the text and photos to help you.

3 In the Guru Granth Sahib God is described in the Mool Mantra.

> **Mool Mantra**
> There is one supreme, absolute God, his name is Eternal Truth.
> God is in all things, he is Creator of all,
> He is without fear, without hatred,
> His existence is timeless, immortal and everywhere.
> He is beyond birth and death, he is self-existent.
> By his grace and goodness people come to know him.

Every Sikh knows this hymn by heart. Discuss the view of God described here. Try to put together a short description of God in your own words.

4 Imagine you are a Sikh explaining about your holy scriptures to a friend who is not Sikh. Write about the place and importance of the Guru Granth Sahib for Sikhs.

5 Religious people turn to their holy book to find comfort and guidance. Find readings from different scriptures and other books which might be helpful in the following circumstances.
   - When someone is sad
   - When someone is making a difficult decision
   - When someone is feeling they can't cope with life's problems.

6 Build a model of the takht with the stool and canopy in the gurdwara out of a box or card. Use silken material and coloured decorations to make it complete.

40

Community and equality

One of the essential features of Sikhism is the community of worshippers. This is called the **sangat**. The sangat is based on the belief that all people are equal in the sight of God. There are no divisions of caste or status. The community elects a group of their members to see to the running of the gurdwara. Someone is also chosen to be responsible for the reading of the scriptures. He or she is called the **granthi**. The granthi has no special privilege or status. They will have a sound knowledge and understanding of the Guru Granth Sahib. The life of the sangat is centred round the gurdwara. Gurdwara means 'door' or 'house' to the guru.

It is the name given to any building where the scriptures are installed. In India the gurdwara is often an impressive building. In Britain, many gurdwaras are converted churches, halls or even cinemas. The main room of the gurdwara is the prayer hall where the Guru Granth Sahib is installed and where **diwan** or public worship is held (A). Sikhs shower or wash before arriving at the gurdwara. This is the way of preparing the mind and body for worship. On entering, the worshippers remove their shoes. This keeps the carpets clean for sitting on and is a sign of respect. When Sikhs enter for worship they go first to bow before the Guru Granth Sahib and leave a small gift of money or food. Then they find a place to sit. Sikhs try not to show disrespect to the holy book by turning their backs irreverently or sitting with their feet sticking out towards it. Men and women often sit separately for worship but this is just social custom.

A   *A prayer hall of a gurdwara*

40

Community and equality

Worship at the gurdwara begins with a reading from the Guru Granth Sahib. The granthi carefully lets the pages fall open and from that page the text is chosen for the day. The granthi chants the reading in Punjabi. The congregation joins in with the well known hymns. These are accompanied by the musicians on the harmonium and **tabla**. During the service the granthi ceremonially waves the chauri above the pages of the scriptures. Sometimes there is a sermon and notices are read out. As the service draws to a close, prayers from the words of Guru Nanak are recited and the congregation stands. With hands together and heads bowed they join in the closing prayer, called the **Ardas**. The word **Waheguru** meaning 'Wonderful Lord' is repeated several times, in reverence and praise. To one side of the takht there is a bowl of sweet, hot pudding called **karah parshad**. It is made from equal quantities of flour, butter, sugar and water under the strictest conditions of purity. Prayers are said over the mixture and it is cut with a kirpan. A small portion is set near the Guru Granth Sahib for the granthi. The rest is shared out among the worshippers (B). It is a symbol of God's grace and blessing to all.

THINGS TO DO

1. The community is very important in the Sikh faith. How can you tell this from what you have learnt? What is a community? Discuss this and then make a chart to show the different communities you and members of your class belong to.

2. Food is often a symbol of spiritual nourishment. We sometimes talk about food for thought. Religions show that humans need to be fed, not only in body and mind but in spirit too. How can the human soul or spirit be nourished? Discuss this question in class. Make a symbolic design of the different ways we need feeding, showing physical food, food for thought and spiritual food.

3. The hymns of the Guru Granth Sahib are set to music. Do you remember the words of songs more easily than readings? Why do you think Guru Nanak travelled with a musician? In your own words write a few sentences about music in the gurdwara and draw the harmonium and tabla.

4. Sikhs believe that all are equal in the eyes of God and no one is more valuable than anyone else. How do they show this? Is it important that we recognize that all human beings are equally valuable? Are there occasions when people are treated as though they were not valuable? Discuss this in class.

5. To make karah parshad, equal parts of flour, sugar and butter are cooked until golden brown. Then the same weight in water is added. This mixture is cooked until it becomes thick like a pudding. Make karah parshad and try it at home as a dessert or try it in your class at school. What do you think the sweetness of the mixture represents?

6. Imagine you are arranging a class trip to a service at the gurdwara. Write a short information sheet describing what to expect, what to look for and how to behave.

B *Karah parshad*

41
A place for worship

The Sikh community gives the impression of being like a large family. The worshippers pray together, they also cook and eat together. Every gurdwara has a **langar** or kitchen. After worship the congregation shares a community meal, also called **langar** (A). Worshippers bring gifts of money and food so the gurdwara can provide food free to visitors (B). Families volunteer each week to prepare langar. It is a great honour to serve the community. **Sewa** or service is an essential part of Sikh life. In parts of India, where caste still influences the way of life, it is unusual for people from different backgrounds to eat together. In Guru Nanak's time it would have been seen as a threat to the normal way of things, a protest against the system.

A *Preparing langar*

The **gurdwara** has always been a centre serving the community at large. In India there are many hospitals, schools and charity programmes set up by Sikh foundations. In Britain the gurdwara is a community centre too. The homeland of the Sikh faith is the Punjab region in the North West of the Indian sub-continent. In 1947 the border between India and the new state of Pakistan was drawn up. It cut right through the Punjab leaving many Sikh families uprooted. Some came to Britain. Others found work in East Africa before coming here. Many went to Canada and the USA. The majority of young Sikhs here are British by birth. Their parents and grandparents will speak Punjabi. Young Sikhs may speak Punjabi at home but at school they learn to read and write in English. The gurdwara may provide lessons in Punjabi so that their mother tongue is not lost and they can understand the scriptures. Some gurdwaras involve their young people in the life of the community by encouraging them to learn to play the tabla and harmonium and many gurdwaras now run youth clubs.

The gurdwara provides a vital link for the older generation so they can keep in touch with their faith and tradition. It is a meeting place and central point in the life of the community.

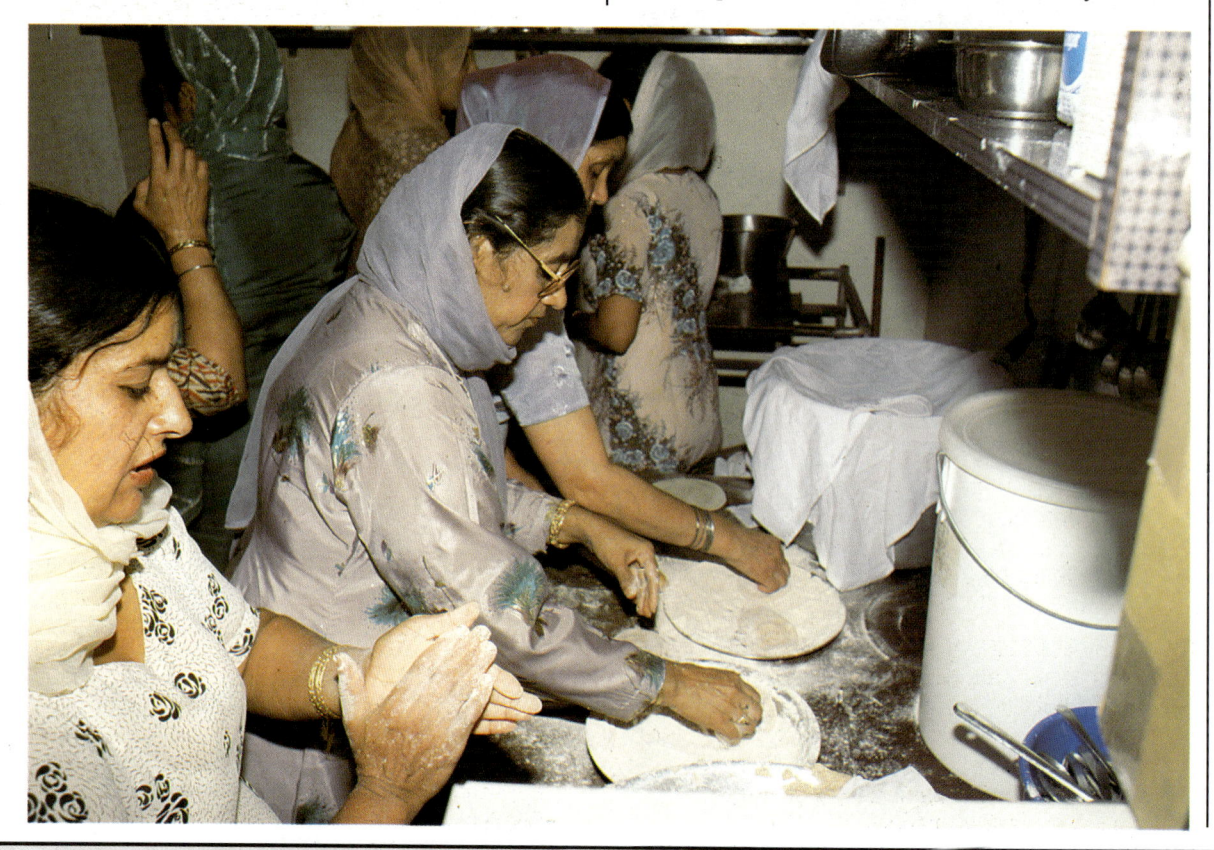

41
A place for worship

B *Offerings at the foot of the Guru Granth Sahib*

THINGS TO DO

1. Langar is a demonstration of how people can share and eat together in trust and friendship no matter what the differences in background. It is a way of acting out the belief that all are equal and acceptable in the eyes of God. It also provides for those in need. Design a poster which invites people to langar after the Sikh service.

2. Sikh children learn about the courage of the gurus in the past who were prepared to face all kinds of danger in the name of justice. Guru Arjun suffered torture and death rather than give into oppression. Find out more about the **Ten Gurus** and their struggle against evil and injustice.

3. If young Sikhs are to understand their scriptures they need to learn to read and write Punjabi. There are other reasons for young Sikhs to learn the language. Write a short play in which Sikh parents are trying to encourage their son or daughter to attend Punjabi lessons.

4. Look at Photo A of langar. Imagine you are Sikh and you are taking a friend who is not Sikh along to the gurdwara for the service and langar. Explain the meaning of the service and langar for you.

5. There are many things in the teachings of the great religions from which we can learn. What do you think Sikhism can teach us? Write your answers and then discuss them.

6. A Sikh prayer reads: 'O Lord, you are the father and the mother, we are your children. Nobody knows your bounds, O Lord. You are supreme.' What does this tell you about Sikhism?

42
Daily life

A *Sikhs at prayer*

According to Sikhism, God is to be found in everyday life. No one should be expected to give up their work or family in order to find God. Earning an honest living and bringing up a family can be an act of service and a form of worship. Every action can be an act of praise if it is carried out in God's name. Guru Nanak taught, 'He alone has found the right way who eats what he has earned through toil and shares his earnings with others.' Sikhs are expected to work hard and put aside 10 per cent of their income for the poor. No work is considered unclean or unworthy as long as it is honest and causes no harm to others.

Devout Sikhs rise very early in the morning when the world is quiet. They shower or bathe before reciting their dawn prayers (A). These are the words of Guru Nanak found in the **Japji**. It reminds Sikhs that love of God is more important than anything else. 'Listen my heart, love God ceaselessly as a fish loves water.'

Some Sikhs go to the gurdwara early to hear the Guru Granth Sahib. Sikhs try to keep God in mind constantly. The Guru Granth Sahib teaches: 'The guru's disciple who with each breath and every morsel of food contemplates the Lord God becomes pleasing to the Guru's mind.'

Food in the Sikh home varies from family to family. Some Sikhs choose to be vegetarian, although there is no religious requirement to avoid meat. Most Sikhs do not eat beef. This is probably due to the Indian background of the faith. In the evening many Sikhs attend the gurdwara to hear the reading from the Guru Granth Sahib. The pattern of worship is fitted around the working day where possible. Sikhs remember God's name again and recite words from the scriptures at the close of the day. Children learn the way of their faith from the example of their parents. Often grandparents, too, play an important part in bringing up the

42
Daily life

B *Sikh children learning Punjabi*

C *Nishan sahib outside the gurdwara*

The Sikh symbol

children. They may tell them stories from the lives of the gurus and teach them to recite well loved prayers from the scriptures. Children may be encouraged to join in activities and classes at the gurdwara as well as work hard at school (B). Like parents in all religions, Sikh parents feel that by passing on their faith to their sons and daughters they are giving them the best possible preparation for life.

THINGS TO DO

1. Sikhs consider education, work and family life to be very important, and that religion should not be separate from life. Write an article for a magazine or paper called 'A Day in the Life of a Sikh' from the Sikh point of view.

2. Look at Photo B of the Sikh children. Imagine you are a Sikh attending classes in Punjabi at the gurdwara. What would you like about it? What would you not like so much?

3. Giving to charity and serving the community are important to the Sikh way of life. In India this service might take the form of providing water for thirsty travellers or helping with langar. In Britain Sikhs help at the gurdwara, cleaning, serving langar, teaching Punjabi, etc. Design a leaflet or letter asking for volunteers to help in this way.

4. The true Sikh should keep God's holy name in his heart and mind at all times. It is often hard to remember God all the time. Why do you think this is? Discuss this in class.

5. The way of life we are used to in our home and family is very important. It makes us feel safe and comfortable when other things around us are new or changing. It is therefore very important that we are not made to feel ashamed or embarrassed about our family life and culture. What things make you feel safe and secure? Write a paragraph or two about this.

6. Study Photo C. Outside the gurdwara there is a flag called the **Nishan sahib**. It has a symbol of a two-edged sword and two curved swords with a circle. These are symbolic. They remind Sikhs to be ready to fight against evil and temptation and to be ready to stand up for the truth. The circle is a symbol of God, without beginning or end. Draw the flag and write a sentence or two about it.

43 Commitment and courage

A Guru Gobind Singh

Sikhs believe that everyone has a soul. The soul lives through many different forms of life before being born into a human body. The aim of the Sikh is to enter the presence of God and at death to become one with him. It is only in human existence that the soul has the opportunity to search out the love of God and seek his presence. Human life is therefore very precious. Sikhs believe that it is God who takes the first step in awakening the human soul to his love. It is God, too, who enlightens the mind to knowledge of the Truth. The Guru Granth Sahib encourages the believer to respond with love and praise: 'In the garden of the heart plant like a seed the word of the Guru and water your garden with love, and all your orchards shall bear the precious fruit of the Holy Name of God.'

In every religion there are some followers who are very deeply committed and others who simply continue the customs and rituals of their family tradition. In Sikhism it is a sign of a person's commitment if they wear the **five Ks**. These symbols of the faith go back to **Guru Gobind Singh** (A). He was the last of the Ten Gurus, a deeply committed man, courageous, educated, upright and courteous. He was able to bring the Sikhs together and give them strength in a time of persecution. He called all the followers of The Gurus to an assembly on the Indian festive occasion of Baisakhi in 1699. He asked for volunteers who would be willing to face his sword and lose their lives for the faith. The followers sat silent and stunned; at first, no one came forward. At last one man rose and went with Guru Gobind Singh into his tent. The guru returned with his sword dripping with blood. Many people slipped away, but one by one four others went into the tent, willing to surrender their lives for the faith. At the end of this time of testing Guru Gobind Singh brought out the five courageous men alive. He gave them **amrit**, water sweetened with sugar and blessed with verses recited from the scriptures. They became the first members of the Sikh **khalsa**, the Pure Ones. They were required to wear the five Ks as a sign of their faith and were given a strict code of conduct: to follow the teachings of the Gurus, to offer daily prayers, to give to charity, to avoid tobacco and alcohol, to be faithful in marriage, to avoid the ritual practices of other religions and to wear the five Ks (B).

The well kept, uncut, clean hair of the Sikh is a symbol of commitment and a reminder of the purity and orderliness required in the life of a Sikh. The comb holds the hair in place. It reminds the Sikh of the need for self-discipline. The shorts replaced the long cloth traditionally worn in India and they too are a reminder of the importance of purity and self-discipline. The kara or bracelet, the unending circle, is a symbol of the unity and eternity of God. The symbol of the sword, often worn as a badge or pendant, is a mark of dignity and fearlessness in the fight against evil, injustice and oppression.

43
Commitment and courage

> **THINGS TO DO**

1. Act out the story of Guru Gobind Singh in class. Discuss the purpose of the guru's actions.

2. Persecution has been a part of the experience of every world religion. It can be felt in a thoughtless hurtful remark or it can be seen in the horrors of the Nazi persecution of the Jews. The vandalism and attacks on places of worship in this country are seen as a form of persecution. Do you think they are? Discuss this.

3. Sikhs are asked to avoid meaningless rituals. Guru Nanak said that it was what was in a person's heart that mattered, not the outward rituals of religion. Is this true? List examples of occasions when rituals are a help and when they become meaningless. Discuss them in class.

4. Guru Gobind Singh gave the five Pure Ones outward symbols as reminders of their commitment to God. He also gave them a set of guidelines by which to live. Symbols and beliefs and concepts are two important aspects of a religion. What other things do most religions have? Copy the diagram below and enter your own ideas to show the different aspects of a religion.

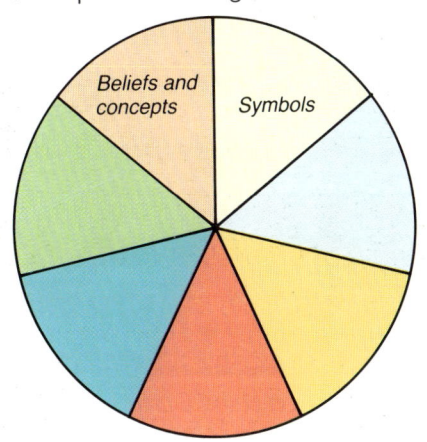

C   *Aspects of religion*

5. Within every religion some believers are very deeply committed, while others do not feel so involved. What would you look for in a deeply committed religious person?

6. Find out more about Guru Gobind Singh and his contribution to the Sikh faith. Write up his story and illustrate it.

B   *Sikhs wearing the ceremonial dress with the five Ks*

44 Renewal and celebration

Baisakhi is New Year's Day in the Punjab region of India. It falls on 13 April. Originally it was a Hindu grain festival. To keep the attention of Sikhs on their own tradition and faith and to discourage them from lapsing into old ways, Baisakhi was made a festival to remember the birth of the khalsa. Today Baisakhi is a political as well as a religious occasion. Elections are held for the gurdwara committees. In India Sikhs travel to the **Golden Temple** in **Amritsar** to bathe in the waters there and to hear the reading from the Guru Granth Sahib. Baisakhi celebrations in Britain are often marked by a complete and unbroken reading of the Guru Granth Sahib. This is called the **Akhand Path** (B). The gurdwara is kept open through the night and **karah parshad** is served to worshippers who come to listen. At the completion of the reading, on the morning of Baisakhi, the gurdwara will be packed with worshippers. A service is held to remember the courage of the first five members of the khalsa. It is an opportunity for everyone to renew their own commitment to the faith.

Baisakhi is not the only special day in the Sikh calendar. Sikhs celebrate the birthday of Guru Nanak and other gurus. These are called **gurpurbs**. They also commemorate anniversaries of those who were martyred. On these occasions there is usually an Akhand Path and in India there is sometimes a procession of the Guru Granth Sahib.

The Hindu festivals of **Divali** and **Holi** have also been reinterpreted by the Sikh faith. At Divali Sikhs remember when the sixth guru gained release from prison and secured the release of 52 Hindus at the same time. This story shows the open-minded and generous nature of the Sikh attitude to people of other faiths. At the spring festival of Holi, Sikhs celebrate **Hola Mohalla** to remember former battles in the face of oppression. It is usually celebrated with military parades, archery contests, fairs, carnivals and processions with flags. At Anandpur, there is an elephant parade to mark the occasion. Many Sikhs in India try to get to the Golden Temple at Amritsar for festive occasions. Amritsar has become a symbol for the Sikh community. It is the centre of their spiritual homeland and for many the land of their families, their culture and history.

A *A procession of the Guru Granth Sahib*

The creation of the Sikh **khalsa** marked a turning in the history of Sikhism. There is a special celebration each year to mark this occasion (A). The festival is called **Baisakhi** and it provides an opportunity for all Sikhs to renew their commitment to the faith and to remember the courage and faith of Sikhs in the past who have set them an example to follow.

44
Renewal and celebration

B *Reading the Guru Granth Sahib*

THINGS TO DO

1. Imagine you are a member of the committee of your local gurdwara. Make a poster to advertise Baisakhi celebrations there.

2. A festival unites a community. How does it do this? Look at the Sikh examples. What special days do the following communities celebrate and what is the meaning of the celebration?
   - a school
   - a family
   - a country
   - a religion

3. Sikhs have had to fight for their freedom to worship during times of persecution. Despite their stormy history the aim of Sikhs is to find peace in union with God. What aspects of Sikhism demonstrate the desire for peace?

4. Sikhism has adapted some of the festivals of the Hindu calendar and given them new meaning. Religions recognize that people need times for rejoicing as well as times for reflection. Do you think we need festivities and celebrations? Why? What festivals do members of your class celebrate?

5. Invite a Sikh to talk about their faith. Prepare a set of questions to ask. Write a letter explaining what you have learnt about Sikhism and what you want to know.

6. Arrange a class visit to a Sikh gurdwara. Take a packet of tea or sugar or biscuits to give to the langar. Remember you will have to cover your heads in the presence of the Guru Granth Sahib. You will also have to remove your shoes. Write an article for a newspaper called 'A visit to a gurdwara'.

45
Room for dialogue

There are important and essential differences between the various religious communities. Sometimes such differences have led to conflict or persecution. People have argued that it would be better if there were no religions at all, then there would be no disagreement and conflict between them. It is true that some of the most bitter conflicts between peoples have been in the name of religion. However, if religion has brought out the worst in some people it has brought out the best in others. There have been devout and committed believers from all of the religions who have lived unselfish lives dedicated to the service of others.

There are of course many people who do not belong to any religious faith or community, who devote their lives to helping those in need and who set an example of unselfishness and generosity. Good deeds are not found only among the religious believers. Humanists do not believe in God or any divine power. Nevertheless they do believe that people should work towards the highest good.

Despite the differences between the various groups there are significant concerns they have in common. Each one of the religions is concerned to show that there can be meaning in life. They all offer a path that leads to a life that is real, meaningful and which promises fulfilment, if not in this life then in another. All the religions teach a way which contrasts with a life based on satisfying purely physical and material desires.

Each of the different religions recognizes the value of prayer or meditation. Most of the religious traditions encourage community worship or practice. In all the religions there is an important place given to sacred writings and traditions. Some religions respect or honour a founding figure, leader or teacher; others revere someone who embodies the truth in human form. These are some of the ways in which points of similarity can be found between the different religions. They are starting points for greater understanding.

There are people and groups who try to bring about greater understanding between people of different religions (A). One of these is the

A *An interfaith service*

45
Room for dialogue

Interfaith Movement in Britain, another is Neve Shalom. Neve Shalom is a project in Israel which aims to bring together Jews, Christians and Muslims (B).

It is hard enough understanding someone who holds beliefs similar to ones own. It is even more difficult to understand someone who has completely different beliefs. One of the most important skills needed in studying religion is the ability to withold judgement in order to be open and fair in coming to understand the beliefs and practices of others. Only then can we let believers explain themselves without feeling judged or criticized. Once we have listened and asked questions and thought carefully, then we can begin to decide whether we agree or disagree with what they are saying. Then it may be that people of different beliefs can learn something from one another.

THINGS TO DO

1. All the religions we have looked at have an important place for their sacred writings. For some the scriptures are of central importance. Make a chart to show the place and importance of the scriptures within each religion.

2. The World Congress of Faiths is a society which tries to bring together leaders and representatives of the different religions. It encourages discussion and tries to break down barriers of mistrust and prejudice between people of different faiths. Find out more about their aims and their work. Write and ask for information from The World Congress of Faiths, 28 Powis Gardens, London W11 1JG. Design a poster for them advertising their work.

3. List the things you think the different religions have in common. With a friend, go down your list and discuss the differences between the religions on each point.

4. Some people argue that religions do more harm than good. Use this as a starting point for a class debate. Have a president, two speakers *for* the motion and two *against*. Take a vote at the end of the lesson.

5. One of the most important skills needed in studying religion is the ability to interpret the meaning behind the outward rituals, symbols and words of religious expression. Take 10 photographs in the book which show religious practices or symbols. Cover up the text. Try to write a sentence or two about each photograph, explaining what is happening in the picture and the meaning behind it.

6. Many people feel that there is no need for religious education in schools as most people do not belong to any particular religion. Is this true? Do you think that RE is important? Discuss your answer with a partner. Compare the different views in class.

B *Neve Shalom*

Glossary

A
Adhan   Muslim call to prayer
Advent   time of preparation leading up to Christmas
Akhand Path   complete and uninterrupted reading of the Guru Granth Sahib
Aleynu   closing prayer of a synagogue service
Allah   Islamic word for God
Alms   charity: gift of food
Altar   table in a church representing the table of the Last Supper
Ambaji   Hindu mother goddess
Amidah   'standing prayer', Jewish prayer said at all services
Amritsar   city and centre of the Sikh homeland in the Punjab
Anglican   belonging to the Church of England, the state church in this country
Ardas   Sikh prayer said at Gurdwara service
Ark   cupboard in the synagogue containing the scriptures also known as the Aron Hakodesh
Arti   offering of light in Hindu worship
Aryans   early invaders into the Indian subcontinent
Ascension Day   Christian festival celebrating Christ's last appearance in human form before his ascension into heaven

B
Baisakhi   Sikh festival celebrating the founding of the Khalsa
Baptism   ceremony involving immersion in water representing the start of a new life; a Christian initiation ceremony
Baptist Church   a church which separated itself from the Church of England because it does not agree with infant baptism
Baptistry   pool for baptism in Baptist church
Bhakti   the path of love followed by hindus; devotion to God
Bhagavad Gita   'Song of the Lord', most popular of Hindu scriptures
Bhajan   Hindu hymn of praise
Bhikkhu   Buddhist monk
Bhikkhuni   Buddhist nun
Bible   the Christian scriptures
Bimah   reading desk in synagogue for reading the scriptures
Bodhisatta   Buddhist saintly being who helps people reach enlightenment
Brahma   Hindu god of creation
Brahman   the Supreme Spirit of the Universe; God
Brahmin   Hindu priest: priestly class in Hindu society
Buddha   Enlightened One: in particular Gotama Buddha

C
Caliph   successor, refers to those who continued the work of Muhammad (Pbuh) as a leader after his death
Catholic   *see* Roman Catholic
Canaan   the land promised to the Israelites as a homeland, now in Israel
Chalice   cup or goblet used in the Christian service of the Lord's Supper
Chauri   fan used to show honour and respect
Christ   'Anointed One' or 'King' (Hebrew Messiah): title given to Jesus by his followers
Christmas   Christian celebration of birth of Jesus Christ
Church   the community of followers of Jesus Christ: a body of Christians: a building used for Christian worship
Commmunion   *see* Holy Communion
Confession   words or thoughts asking for God's forgiveness in private prayer or said in a service or to priest
Consecrate   to make sacred or holy with a blessing performed by a priest
Covenant   sacred agreement between God and his people
Crucifix   Christian symbol of Christ on the cross

D
Deity   god or image of a god
Dhamma   the teachings of the Buddha
Dharma   Hindu word for religion meaning 'what is right' or law
Disciple   follower or learner taught by a teacher: in Christian sense follower of Jesus
Divali   Hindu festival of light
Diwan   Sikh congregational worship
Dussehra   'Ten Days', a Hindu festival dedicated to Durga
Durga   one aspect of the Hindu mother Goddess

E
Easter   the most important Christian festival celebrating the resurrection of Christ
Ecumenical Movement   a Christian movement to try to bring different churches together
Enlightenment   liberation from the bonds of earthly life; a translation of Moksha or Nibbana
Eid ul Adha   Muslim festival of sacrifice
Eid ul Fitr   Muslim festival of fast-breaking
Ephiphany   Christian festival which focuses on the wise men visiting the Christ child
Eucharist   'thanksgiving': Christian service where bread and wine are shared also known as Mass, Holy Communion and the Lord's Supper or the Breaking of Bread

F
Fast   to go without food or certain types of food and drink as a religious duty
Father, Son and Holy Spirit   the three aspects of the Christian Godhead
Five Ks   five religious symbols worn by Sikhs
Font   container for water in a Christian church, used in baptism

G
Ganesha   a Hindu god
Gayatri Mantra   Hindu prayer for enlightenment
Gift of tongues   words or sounds uttered in praise by those 'moved by the Holy Spirit' in Christian worship
Gospel   'Good News' meaning the good news about Jesus Christ; name given to first four books of the New Testament
Good Friday   a day when Christians remember the death of Christ on the cross
Granthi   the leader in Sikh worship who reads the scriptures
Gurdwara   Sikh place of worship

Glossary

Guru   religious or spiritual teacher
Guru Granth Sahib   the Sikh Holy Scriptures
Guru Nanak   the first of the Sikh founders
Guru Gobind Singh   the founder of the Sikh khalsa

H
Hadith   collection of the sayings and actions of the prophet Muhammad
Hafiz   someone who has learnt the Qur'an by heart
Hajj   fifth pillar of Islam, the Pilgrimage to Makkah
Halal   permitted meat slaughtered according to Islamic law
Hallah   special white bread for the Jewish Shabbat meal
Hazzan   the one who leads the chanting in synagogue prayer, also known as a cantor
Havan   Hindu ritual fire
Havdalah   Jewish prayer at the close of Shabbat
Hijrah   the journey Muhammad made from Makkah to Madinah
Holy Communion   Christian service with bread and wine
Holy Spirit   the power and presence of God on earth according to Christian belief
Host   bread or wafer used in Christian Holy Communion to represent the body of Christ
Hola Moholla   Sikh spring festival
Holi   Hindu spring festival

I
Ibrahim   for Muslims a prophet of Allah: Jews and Christians call him Abraham
Imam   leader of prayer in Muslim public worship
Israel   the worldwide community of Jews: the land of Israel: the modern state of Israel

J
Janamashtami   Hindu festival celebrating the birth of Krishna
Japji   words of Guru Nanak, hymn used in Sikh daily prayer
Jati   traditional Hindu social group according to family and occupation
Jum'ah   Muslim Friday midday prayers with sermon

K
Ka'ba   the sacred building dedicated to Allah in Makkah
Kach   shorts worn by Sikhs, one of the five Ks
Kali   one form of the Hindu mother Goddess
Kangha   comb worn by Sikhs, one of the five Ks
Kara   steel band or bracelet worn by Sikhs
Karah parshad   blessed sweet pudding shared out at end of Sikh service at the gurdwara
Kathina   robe giving ceremony for Buddhist monks
Kesh   uncut hair, symbol worn by Sikh
Ketuvim   Jewish sacred writings in the Tenakh
Khalsa   the community of the 'Pure Ones'; the Sikh brotherhood
Khanda   double edged sword symbol on Sikh flag
Kiddush   Jewish blessing or prayer at start of Shabbat
Kirpan   symbolic sword worn by Sikhs
Kosher   food that is 'fit' to eat according to Jewish law
Krishna   human incarnation of Hindu God Vishnu, Saviour of humankind

L
Langar   kitchen at Sikh gurdwara: community meal at gurdwara after the service
Lay community   ordinary men and women of a religious community who are not priests or monks or nuns
Lectern   a stand for the Bible in church
Lent   period of preparation before Easter
Lord's Prayer   Christian prayer from teaching of Christ
Lord's Supper   Christian service where bread and wine are shared to remember the Last Supper

M
Mahabharata   one of the great epics in the Hindu scriptures
Mahayana   the Great Way: one of the two main branches of Buddhism
Makkah   Mecca, the city where Muhammad was born
Mala   string of beads used in prayer or meditation
Mandala   yantra or pattern used in meditation
Mandir   Hindu temple
Manji sahib   stool holding Sikh scripture
Manna   food from heaven in the story of Exodus
Mantra   a chant used for worship and meditation
Mary   the mother of Jesus, and a Catholic Saint
Mass   Roman Catholic name for Holy Communion
Meditation   a process of disciplining the mind in order to gain spiritual or mental insight or sense of wellbeing
Megillah   scroll of the book of Esther used in Purim service in the Synagogue
Menorah   Jewish seven branched candlestick
Messiah   Hebrew word meaning 'Anointed One' or 'King'
Methodist   non-conformist church i.e. separated itself from the Church of England to reform worship
Mezuzah   tiny scroll containing words of the Torah on the doorpost of Jewish household
Mihrab   niche or alcove in mosque to mark direction of Makkah
Minaret   tower of a mosque from where adhan is called
Moksha   Hindu word for 'salvation' or 'liberation'
Mool Mantra   Guru Nanak's words on God used in Sikh prayer
Monotheism   belief in One God only
Mosque   Muslim place of prayer
Muezzin   one who calls worshippers to prayer in Islam
Muhammad   Allah's messenger, the last and most important Prophet according to Islam

N
Nam   Sikh word for the holy Name of God
Navaratri   Hindu festival of Nine Nights
Nevi'im   Jewish books of the prophets in the Tenakh
New Testament   second part of Christian Bible
Nibbana   'blown out': Buddhist word for liberation from the bonds of earthly life
Night of Power   Muslim festival
Nishan sahib   Sikh flag outside the gurdwara

O
Om   Aum, Hindu sacred sound and symbol used in meditation and worship meaning eternal truth
Old Testament   the first part of the Christian Bible containing the Jewish Tenakh
Orthodox church   those branches of the Christian church which are traditionally found in Russia, Greece and Eastern Europe

P
Passover   *see* Pesach

Glossary

Pentecost fifty days after Pesach on the Jewish calendar; the Christian festival of Whitsun
Parable story told by Jesus which compares spiritual truths with everyday realities
Pesach Jewish festival commemorating the Exodus
Pbuh 'Peace be upon Him'; Muslims put this after the name of Muhammad to show respect
Prashad blessed food
Priest religious leader: in Anglican and Catholic context priests have in ordination received the authority given by Christ to St. Peter
Prophet someone sent by God to speak his message
Protestant those churches which do not accept the authority of the Pope as the head of the Christian community and which do not belong to the Orthodox churches
Puja offerings and acts of devotion at a shrine
Pulpit raised platform from which sermons are given in a church
Purana Hindu scriptures containing stories and myths
Purim Jewish festival

Q

Qur'an the Muslim sacred scriptures
Qiblah the direction of Muslim prayer i.e. towards the Ka'ba in Makkah

R

Rabbi teacher: leader in the Jewish community
Rak'ah a cycle of prayer in Muslim salah
Rama an incarnation of the Hindu God Lord Vishnu
Ramadan the Muslim month of fasting
Ramayana one of the epics of the Hindu scriptures
Rebirth being born into a new life
Reincarnation the belief that the soul survives death to live again in a new body on earth
Resurrection Christian belief that Christ overcame death and is alive today: life after death
Retreat getting away from everyday life for a while to concentrate on prayer, meditation and spiritual life
Revelation something that has been revealed to humankind
Roman Catholic the Christian community that accepts the Pope as the head of the Church
Rosh Hashanah Jewish New Year

S

Sacrament an outward sign or symbolic action carrying a spiritual blessing
Sacrifice an offering that is of personal cost
Saint a being whose life is an example of faith
Salvation Army a Christian evangelical church founded by William Booth
Salah Muslim set prayer
Sangha community of Buddhist monks and nuns
Sanghat the Sikh congregation of worshippers
Sannyasin someone who has given up worldly attachments to seek spiritual truth
Sat Nam the True Name, a Sikh title for God
Saum Muslim fast, one of the five pillars of faith
Saviour one who saves others from evil or death
Sefer Torah the scroll of the Torah in the synagogue
Shabbat Jewish day of rest
Shahadah Muslim declaration of faith
Shema verses from the Jewish Torah containing the core beliefs of the Jewish faith
Shi'ites followers of Ali, a descendant of Muhammad
Shiva Hindu god, Lord of destruction
Shrine a special place, often containing a symbol, image or relic as a focus for worship
Shruti 'revealed' Hindu scriptures
Shudras one of the classes of ancient Hindu society
Simchat Torah Jewish festival celebrating the Torah
Smirti 'remembered' Hindu scriptures: the epics
Society of Friends breakaway church known as Quakers
Surah chapter or division of the Qur'an
Sunni the majority of Muslims, not Shi'ite, who accept the authority of Muhammad's choice of successor but not his descendents
Synagogue Jewish place for gathering for worship

T

Takht platform in gurdwara from where the scriptures are read
Tallit Jewish prayer shawl
Talmud the body of interpretation and discussion of the Jewish Torah
Tenakh the Torah, Nevi'im and Ketuvi'im which make up the Jewish scriptures
Tephilin scrolls in tiny leather boxes containing words from the Torah worn by Jewish men in weekday prayers
Theravada the 'Way of the Elders', the older of the two main branches of Buddhism
Tipitaka the 'three baskets', the collection of Buddhist scriptures of the Pali canon
Torah the five books of Moses, the core of the Jewish scriptures

U

Untouchable a class of Hindu society once thought to be unclean
Uposatha days at full moon and mid-month and quarters of the Buddhist calendar, times of paying special attention to Dhamma

V

Vaishyas one class division of traditional Hindu society
Varna traditional classes or divisions of Hindu society
Vedas most ancient of Hindu revealed scripture
Vesakha Buddhist festival marking the birth, enlightenment and death of the Buddha
Vishnu Hindu god who comes to earth in different forms

W

Wesak *see* Vesakha
Whitsun Christian festival marking the time when the disciples received the Holy Spirit
Wudu ritual washing before Muslim prayer

Y

Yad pointer used to read the Sefer Torah
Yamulka Jewish head covering also known as kapel
Yoga ancient system of exercises for controlling and disciplining the body and senses
Yom Kippur Jewish 'Day of Atonement'

Z

Zakah charity required of all Muslims